THE BOOMER
ARCHAEOLOGIST

THE BOOMER ARCHAEOLOGIST

A Graphic Memoir of Tribes, Identity, and the Holy Land

THOMAS EVAN LEVY

Illustrated by
LILY ALMEIDA

Designed by
BHAVESHKUMAR SURU

SHEFFIELD UK   BRISTOL CT

Published by Equinox Publishing Ltd.

UK: Office 415, The Workstation,
15 Paternoster Row, Sheffield,
South Yorkshire S1 2BX

USA: ISD, 70 Enterprise Drive, Bristol, CT 06010

www.equinoxpub.com

First published 2025

© Thomas Evan Levy 2025

All rights reserved. No part of this publication may be reproduced or transmitted in any form or by any means, electronic or mechanical, including photocopying, recording or any information storage or retrieval system, without prior permission in writing from the publishers.

British Library Cataloguing-in-Publication Data

A catalogue record for this book is available from the British Library.

ISBN-13   918 1 80050 695 4   (paperback)
               918 1 80050 696 1   (ePDF)
               918 1 80050 700 5   (ePub)

Library of Congress Cataloging-in-Publication Data:

Names: Thomas Evan Levy, Author; Lily Almeida, Illustrator; BhaveshKumar Suru, Designer
Title: The Boomer Archaeologist: A Graphic Memoir of Tribes, Identity, and the Holy Land / Thomas Evan Levy; Illustrated by Lily Almeida.
Other titles: Graphic Memoir of Tribes, Identity, and the Holy Land
Description: Sheffield, South Yorkshire; Bristol, CT: Equinox Publishing Ltd, 2025.
Summary: "In this graphic memoir Thomas Evan Levy tells his life story, including 40 years of surveying, excavating and adventure in the deserts of the Holy Land, and then how to 'cool off' he got into marine archaeology. Throughout this story, tribes and identity play both a personal role and a focus of the author's research. This book is illustrated by Lily Almeida" – Provided by publisher.
Identifiers: LCCN 2025000960 (Print); LCCN 2025000961 (E-Book); ISBN 9781800506954 (Paperback); ISBN 9781800506961 (ePDF); ISBN 9781800507005 (ePub).
Subjects: LCSH: Levy, Thomas Evan – Comic books, strips, etc. Archaeologists – United States – Biography – Comic books, strips, etc. I Jews – United States – Biography – Comic books, strips, etc. Archaeology – Middle East – Comic books, strips, etc. LCGFT: Comics (Graphic works) – Autobiographies
Classification: LCC CC115.L48 A3 2025 (Print) I LCC CC115.L48 (E-Book) I DDC 956.0090909 – dc23/eng/20250508
LC record available at https://lccn.loc.gov/2025000960
LC ebook record available at https://lccn.loc.gov/2025000961

Authored by **Thomas Evan Levy** (https://ccas.ucsd.edu)
Cover & interior illustrations by **Lily Almeida** (www.lilydoodles.co.uk)
Cover & layout design, typesetting & formatting by **BhaveshKumar Suru** (www.bksuru.com)
Printed and bound by **CPI Group (UK) Ltd**, Croydon, CR0 4YY

for
Alina

THOMAS EVAN LEVY

◦ ENDORSEMENTS ◦

"A creative and completely unique self-excavation by a gifted archaeologist equally at home in America and the Middle East, in the present and in Biblical times. 'The Boomer Archaeologist' is at once playful, serious, and deeply touching."

~ **MATTI FRIEDMAN (ISRAEL)**
Author of **"Who by Fire: Leonard Cohen in the Sinai"**
(Penguin Random House)

"If there were an award for the most surprising book of the year, I'd nominate 'The Boomer Archeologist.' In this coming-of-age story of the makings of a brilliant archeologist, Tom Levy takes us on an extraordinary journey through desert excavations and underwater digs, exploring ancient civilizations from Israel and Jordan to India and Africa. Along the way he unpacks wider stories — the archeological controversies over the veracity of the biblical narrative, the growing challenges of being an American Jew, the possibilities of friendship and respect between Jews and Arabs. Levy writes with charm and humor and most of all wonder at the adventure that has been his life. One of the most fascinating Jewish autobiographies of our time."

~ **YOSSI KLEIN HALEVI (ISRAEL)**
Senior Fellow, *Shalom Hartman Institute*
Author of the New York Times bestseller,
"Letters to My Palestinian Neighbor"

THE BOOMER ARCHAEOLOGIST
· ENDORSEMENTS ·

"For people of our generation, archaeology was more than just a career. It was a passion fueled by our fascination with the past and how that past can enrich our collective lives. Archaeology combines the love of scientific discovery with history, philosophy, and anthropology. As Levy says, it gives us the intellectual tools to understand the human condition. Tom's delightful book illustrates the joy of archaeology through a lifetime journey of discovery, both personal and scientific. For me, Tom's career and life embody the ideal of the professional archaeologist of any age."

~ **CHARLES (CHIP) STANISH (USA)**
Executive Director at the Institute for the Advanced Study of Culture and Environment, **University of South Florida, Tampa Campus, USA**
Director and Professor Emeritus, **Cotsen Institute of Archaeology at UCLA**

"Tom Levy's 'The Boomer Archeologist' is one of the most charming, entertaining, and intelligent autobiographies I have ever read. Among the leading Eastern Mediterranean archaeologists of our generation, Tom has been a visionary and pioneer in many fields, including the study of early complex societies, the introduction of the exact life sciences to archaeology, ancient metallurgy, and recently, cyber archaeology. Not surprising, this engaging book is also an exception. Tom tells his story, in many ways the story of archaeology in our region, in alluring graphics drawn by Lily Almeida. He does this in a moving personal tone — with wit and emotion, courageously not caching matters of culture and identity. A rare delight."

~ **ISRAEL FINKELSTEIN (ISRAEL)**
Professor and Head of the School of Archaeology and Maritime Cultures, **University of Haifa, Israel**
Member, the **Israel Academy of Sciences and Humanities**
Foreign Member, the **French Académie des Inscriptions et Belles-Lettres**
Foreign Member, **American Academy of Arts and Sciences**

A Graphic Memoir of Tribes, Identity, and the Holy Land
THOMAS EVAN LEVY

"A very personal and entertaining narrative, looking behind the scenes of a life well-lived. Tom Levy's reminiscences of his experiences as a groundbreaking archaeologist are amusing and thought-provoking by turns, and are well worth reading and contemplating by students, specialists, and the general public alike."

~ ERIC H. CLINE (USA)
Professor of Classics, History, and Anthropology
The George Washington University
Author of **"After 1177 B.C.: The Survival of Civilizations"**
(Princeton University Press)

"Levy's graphic memoir is a compelling story of identity, resilience, and global adventure, shaped by his roots as the son of a WWII veteran. From his Californian upbringing to his archaeological work in Israel and Jordan — where he forged groundbreaking partnerships between Jews and Arabs after the 1990s peace accords — and his journeys to India, Greece, and Sheffield, Levy's life exemplifies curiosity and cooperation. Through vibrant illustrations, he reflects on being a proud Jewish American while confronting the rise of antisemitism in academia. A poignant epilogue on October 7th brings added depth to this timely and inspiring memoir."

~ JONATHAN SANDLER (UNITED KINGDOM)
Author of "The English GI: World War II Graphic Memoir"
(GraphicMemoir.co.uk)

THE BOOMER ARCHAEOLOGIST
◦ ENDORSEMENTS ◦

"In this vivid graphic memoir, archaeologist Tom Levy delivers a unique inside view of his decades of groundbreaking discoveries that have transformed our understanding of the ancient Holy Land. He also presents an absorbing personal story of growing up as a Californian boomer and rediscovering his heritage in Israel in the midst of turbulent political events. Highly recommended!"

~ **EVAN HADINGHAM (USA)**
Author of *"Discovering Us"* (Signature Books)
The Leakey Foundation

"This illustrated book by noted anthropologist and Biblical archaeologist Thomas Levy is a unique story about his family, life, and professional career. It's a testimony of the world that used to be and the one we are in these past one hundred years. Levy's contribution to the archaeology of the Near East can't be exaggerated. Enjoy this journey and follow Tom on travels in time and human history through his thoughts and deeds. It will change your perspective of the world we live in."

~ **MIROSLAV BÁRTA (CZECH REPUBLIC)**
Professor & Director, **Czech Institute of Egyptology**
Director of the Abusir Mission, **Charles University, Prague**
Senator, **Parliament of the Czech Republic**

A Graphic Memoir of Tribes, Identity, and the Holy Land
THOMAS EVAN LEVY

"Graphic novels are hardly the stock-in-trade for distinguished scientists. In 'The Boomer Archaeologist', Tom Levy and his niece, the able illustrator Lily Almeida, provide a (literally) colorful journey through Levy's adventurous life in the trenches, with a no-holds-barred look at his personal struggles, Zionism, and the identity politics roiling today's college campuses. An innovative and engaging memoir."

~ ANDREW LAWLER (USA)
Author of "Under Jerusalem: The Buried History of the World's Most Contested City" (Doubleday)

THOMAS EVAN LEVY

• ACKNOWLEDGEMENTS •

Many thanks to Lily Almeida, my loving niece and the graphic artist who did all the beautiful illustrations for my graphic memoir. I'm grateful to several friends who read different versions of this work during its evolution: Yossi Klein Halevi, Sarah Klein Halevi, Evan Hadingham, the late Doug Ramsey, and Matti Friedman.

I would also like to thank Jonathan Sandler for his advice and BhaveshKumar Suru for the excellent design of this book. I'm grateful to my longtime publisher, Janet Joyce, for her willingness to always take a chance with my publication ideas. Thanks also to the Equinox staff for their help in publishing this book: Valerie Hall, Sarah Lee, Daniel Gronow, and Mark Lee. Thanks to my friend Ken Garrett, a National Geographic photographer, who joined me on the Journey to the Copper Age expedition and gave me permission to use his photographs here.

I'm especially grateful to my wonderful and beautiful wife, Alina, for being with me and supporting me in so many ways for most of my story depicted in this memoir. Finally, during the production of this book, my son Gil and Veronica brought our beautiful granddaughter, Ayla, into this world.

THOMAS EVAN LEVY

· CONTENTS ·

Prologue: Rivers in the Desert

1. Early History of the Levys
From Bialystok to Woodbine, NJ

2. World War II with the US 452nd Bomb Group
Howard I. Levy, Serial No. 13-097-882

3. Post-WWII California Dreamin'
1950s in the San Fernando Valley

4. 1960s
In the Valley

5. The Late 1960s
Discovering Anthropology

THE BOOMER ARCHAEOLOGIST
· CONTENTS ·

6. Road to Anthropology
Late 1960s–1970

7. I Am a Jew
A Message to All Minorities, 1969–1971

8. Journey to the Holy Land
Archaeology and Kibbutz, 1971

9. To the Old Pueblo
Discovering Behavioral Archaeology, 1973

10. Sailing the Wine-Dark Sea
Greece, 1973

11. Yom Kippur War, 1973

A Graphic Memoir of Tribes, Identity, and the Holy Land
THOMAS EVAN LEVY

12. Back to Tucson and Back to Home, 1974

13. Licking My Wounds in the Valley, 1974

14. The Road to Prehistory — Final U of A Days, 1975

15. The Full Monty — Early Days in Sheffield, 1976–1977

16. Back to the Holy Land, 1977

17. Copper Age Nirvana and Dad's Death, 1978

THE BOOMER ARCHAEOLOGIST
• CONTENTS •

18. The Man in the Desert Museum — Bedouins, 1979–1985

19. Marriage and Tribe, 1978–1979

20. The People's Army — IDF, 1984–1992

21. East Jerusalem and the W.F. Albright Institute, 1985–1987

22. West Jerusalem and the Nelson Glueck School for Biblical Archaeology, 1987–1992

23. Beautiful Boys — Ben and Gil, 1988

A Graphic Memoir of Tribes, Identity, and the Holy Land
THOMAS EVAN LEVY

24. Warring Chiefdoms from the Banks of the Wadi Beersheva, 1987–1993

25. The Archaeology of Cult: 1987, 1990–1992

26. Terror in Baka, 1990

27. From Ethnoarchaeology in Cameroon to the Gulf War

28. The Golden Medina, 1992

29. Earliest Egyptian Colonization in Canaan, Nahal Tillah, 1994–1996

THE BOOMER ARCHAEOLOGIST
CONTENTS

30. Crossing Jordan, 1997
Jordan-Israel Peace Treaty, October 26, 1994

31. Archaeometallurgy and Cyber-Archaeology in Jordan, 1999

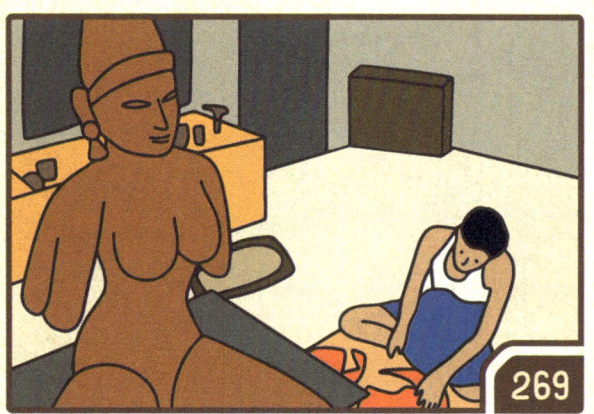

32. Ethnoarchaeology in India, 2004–2007

33. Quest for Solomon's Mines, 2002–2014

34. At-Risk World Heritage and the Oracle at Delphi

35. Underwater Archaeology in Israel

A Graphic Memoir of Tribes, Identity, and the Holy Land
THOMAS EVAN LEVY

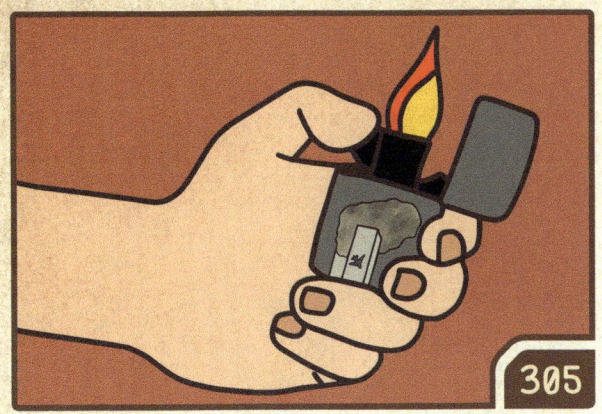

36. The Collapse of Civilizations

Epilogue: Gratitude

Photo Story 1: Shiqmim
The Rise of Social Inequality,
ca. 4500–3600 BCE

Photo Story 2: Gilat
Earliest Temples in the
Holy Land, ca. 4500–3600 BCE

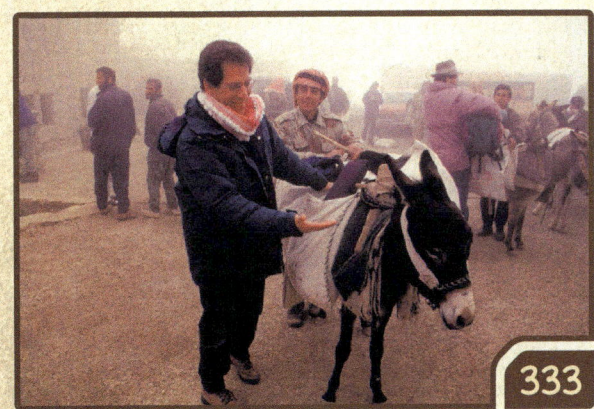

Photo Story 3: Copper Trail
Journey to the Copper Age
Action Archaeology, 1997

Photo Story 4: ELRAP, Jordan
Copper and the Rise of a Biblical Iron
Age Kingdom, 10th–9th Centuries BCE

THE BOOMER ARCHAEOLOGIST
· CONTENTS ·

Photo Story 5: Ethnoarchaeology
The Hereditary Bronze Casters of South India

Photo Story 6: Methoni Bay Marine Archaeology
Cultural Heritage Project, Greece

Photo Story 7: Deep-Time Holocene Coastal Adaptation
Israel and the Earliest Tsunami

Postscript: October 7, 2023

THE BOOMER ARCHAEOLOGIST

THOMAS EVAN LEVY

• PROLOGUE •

Rivers in the Desert

THE BOOMER ARCHAEOLOGIST
· PROLOGUE ·

By the end of November 2009, winter had arrived and the weather in the Jordanian desert was wild. Most, but not all, of our Israeli army tents stood up to the storms.

Rivers in the Desert

As usual, our team woke up around 4:15 a.m. to prepare for the challenging off-road ride out to Khirbat en-Nahas (Ruins of Copper in Arabic) — the Iron Age copper factory that was the focus of my fieldwork with Mohammad Najjar. The morning sky over the Sharah Mountains was still being lit up with lightning strikes.

As the sun rose, my research partner Mohammad Najjar and I went to an overlook to observe the flood coming down the Wadi Fidan. As this would be our first crossing point to get to Khirbat en-Nahas, we decided to wait several hours before starting our journey.

THE BOOMER ARCHAEOLOGIST
• PROLOGUE •

By this time, Mohammad and I had worked together for over 13 years. The drive through the wadi gave me time to reflect; working in Jordan brought so many things in my life together. My desire to contribute toward peace and normal relations between Jews and Arabs on a personal level; my love for Arab and Bedouin culture; my pride in following in the footsteps of the great Jewish-American archaeologist Nelson Glueck — an early explorer in Jordan; and my feeling of being very much at home in the Middle East.

Rivers in the Desert

Little did I know then, our work at Khirbat en-Nahas would soon throw me into fierce academic debates concerning the historicity of Israel's earliest kings — David and Solomon, dating to the 10th century BCE. Some 2 decades earlier, I was embroiled in another archaeological debate — the rise of the first chiefdoms and the early institutionalization of social inequality in the Middle East during the 5th millennium BCE.

KEY:

A – 10th c. BCE gatehouse
F – Copper processing building
R – Elite building
S – Slag processing building
T – Tower
GMM – German Mining Museum probe
M – Slag mound excavation
W – Dwellings

THE BOOMER ARCHAEOLOGIST
◦ PROLOGUE ◦

Why did members of the scholarly community want to confront me? Was it personal? Was it my use of science-based archaeological methods in these contentious epochs? Was it my refusal to accept a literal reading of the Hebrew Bible for my understanding the archaeological record? Or was it my anthropological perspective for interpreting the past that bothered my detractors? Did they take issue with my cross-cultural approach, whereby sites and cultures in the Holy Land, a unique place on the planet, could be understood in relation to those in other parts of the world?

Thanks Lily! You'll see in my story, besides working as a paperboy and a few phases as a "cowboy," I've been blessed to be an archaeologist and do archaeology all my life. I'll tell you about my 40 years of surveying, excavating, and adventuring in the deserts of the Holy Land, and then how, to "cool off," I got into marine archaeology. Throughout this story, tribes and identity play both a personal role and a focus of my research. In fact, tribalism underlies all societies even today. OK Lily, let's dive into my story…

THE BOOMER ARCHAEOLOGIST

THOMAS EVAN LEVY

CHAPTER 1

Early History of the Levys

From Bialystok to Woodbine, NJ

THE BOOMER ARCHAEOLOGIST
· CHAPTER 1 ·

Late 1800s: Anti-Jewish pogroms in the Russian Empire led my grandparents — the Levys and Goldmans — to flee Europe.

The Levys ended up in Woodbine, New Jersey, a utopian Jewish agricultural settlement set up by Baron de Hirsch.

Early History of the Levys
From Bialystok to Woodbine, NJ

"I shall try to make for them a new home in different lands, where, as free farmers, on their own soil, they can make themselves useful to the country."

~ Baron Maurice de Hirsch, August 1891.

THE BOOMER ARCHAEOLOGIST
◦ CHAPTER 1 ◦

By the late 1930s, my dad, Howard, and his 4 siblings worked in their father Abraham's dry-goods store in Woodbine.

November 1938: A pogrom called Kristallnacht (Night of the Broken Glass) was organized in Germany by the Nazi paramilitary and civilians against German Jews. About 7,000 Jewish businesses were damaged or destroyed, and 30,000 Jewish men were arrested and incarcerated in concentration camps.

Early History of the Levys
From Bialystok to Woodbine, NJ

The Levy children, from oldest to youngest, were: Ruth (Ruthie, b. 1920), Jacob (Jay, b. 1922), Howard (Hotchie, b. 1923), Doris (Doshie, b. 1925), and Betty (b. 2018). When I did my "23andMe" genetic testing, I discovered I was 98% Ashkenazi Jewish and 2% Neanderthal. That means the family of my mother Phyllis Magill (née Mogolovski) also came from the same general area as my father's family. After WWII, most Jews could not imagine not marrying a fellow Jew — someone from the same tribe!

The morning after Kristallnacht, 15-year-old Howard went up to his parents' attic and smashed the family's Passover china set made in Germany. ✡

CHAPTER 2

World War II with the US 452nd Bomb Group

Howard I. Levy, Serial No. 13-097-882

THE BOOMER ARCHAEOLOGIST
▫ CHAPTER 2 ▫

DAD ENLISTED IN THE US ARMY AIR FORCES IN JULY, 1942. BY NOVEMBER 6, HE DID PARACHUTE TRAINING AT A BASE IN EPHRATA, WASHINGTON STATE.

It is politically incorrect to say it today, however, my father enlisted in the US Army Air Forces because he wanted to kill the Germans. By 1941, the atrocities and growing genocides of the Nazis against Europe's Jewish population was well known. However, Germany's war against the Jews was mostly suppressed by the mainstream media in the USA and rarely mentioned on the front page of leading newspapers.

World War II with the US 452ⁿᵈ Bomb Group
Howard I. Levy, Serial No. 13-097-882

As a 19-year-old, my father was assigned to the 452nd Bomb Group and the 729th Squadron, whose unofficial cartoon logo was a wolf holding a bomb and riding a B-17. They trained together for a year in the USA before being sent to Europe. Dad got into a fight at one of the US training bases when someone called him a "dirty Jew." This postponed his advancement to the rank of Sergeant, which he finally earned when the 452nd was stationed in England.

THE BOOMER ARCHAEOLOGIST
◦ CHAPTER 2 ◦

A train from Scotland took Dad and his bomb group to Deopham Green Air Field in Norfolk, England, where he served as an armorer and a waist gunner on a B-17 for 1.5 years.

APRIL 13, 1944: DAD EARNS 1 OF HIS 8 BATTLE STARS

Toward the end of WWII, Dad was transferred from England to ground forces in Europe.

On April 29, he helped liberate the Dachau Concentration Camp in Germany. According to my father, the American liberators were told to administer "instant justice" to the Nazi troops they encountered. This was something he never told my mother, he only revealed it to me just a week before he died in 1978. The experiences of WWII no doubt influenced my father's strong belief that Jews should be armed wherever they lived, including in the USA. In retrospect, my father must have suffered from Post-Traumatic Stress Disorder (PTSD) — something that deeply affected his subsequent choices in life.

THOMAS EVAN LEVY

• CHAPTER 3 •

Post-WWII California Dreamin'

1950s in the San Fernando Valley

THE BOOMER ARCHAEOLOGIST
▫ CHAPTER 3 ▫

HOWARD LEVY AT KIMPO AIR BASE, KOREA, 1950

After WWII, Dad was sure America would never go to war again, so he signed up for the reserves, only to be called up for the Korean War in 1950, at 27 years of age. Mom and Dad got married in 1946, and very soon they unofficially adopted Mom's little 5-year-old brother, Stephen — who, as an infant, had been put into an orphanage by his father, George — soon after his wife, Eva, died, 10 days after giving birth to "Steve."

Post-WWII California Dreamin'
1950s in the San Fernando Valley

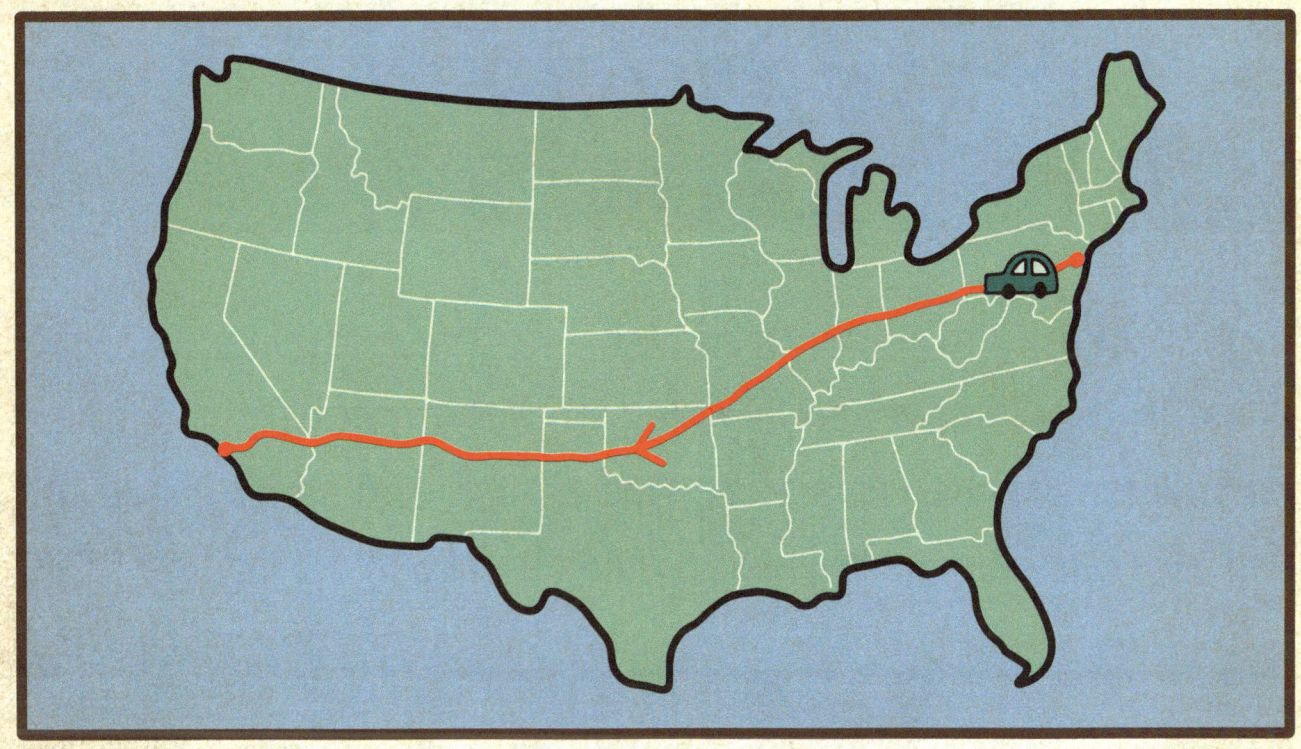

Dad was a tough guy. After he got back from Korea, he got a job offer in 1951 from the Philadelphia mob. This was a wake-up call for Dad, Mom, and Stephen to get out of town and drive to Los Angeles for a new life.

THE BOOMER ARCHAEOLOGIST
· CHAPTER 3 ·

A year after my parents moved into their Marklein Avenue home in the San Fernando Valley, on September 11, 1953, I was born. When Stephen was 14, he was a punk, and so he joined the Drifters Car Club. We enjoyed a suburban bliss during the 1950s.

Our family boxer dog, Rex, was my guardian angel. Rex slept at my bedroom door, always on guard duty.

Post-WWII California Dreamin'
1950s in the San Fernando Valley

Stephen joined the Drifters Car Club when I was 5. He would incessantly polish his 1949 Chevy convertible that my dad had bought him — even before he had a driver's license.

THE BOOMER ARCHAEOLOGIST
- CHAPTER 3 -

For laughs, Stephen and the Drifters liked to encourage me, a 5-year-old, to smoke cigarettes. They considered this great fun while waxing the Chevy.

Post-WWII California Dreamin'
1950s in the San Fernando Valley

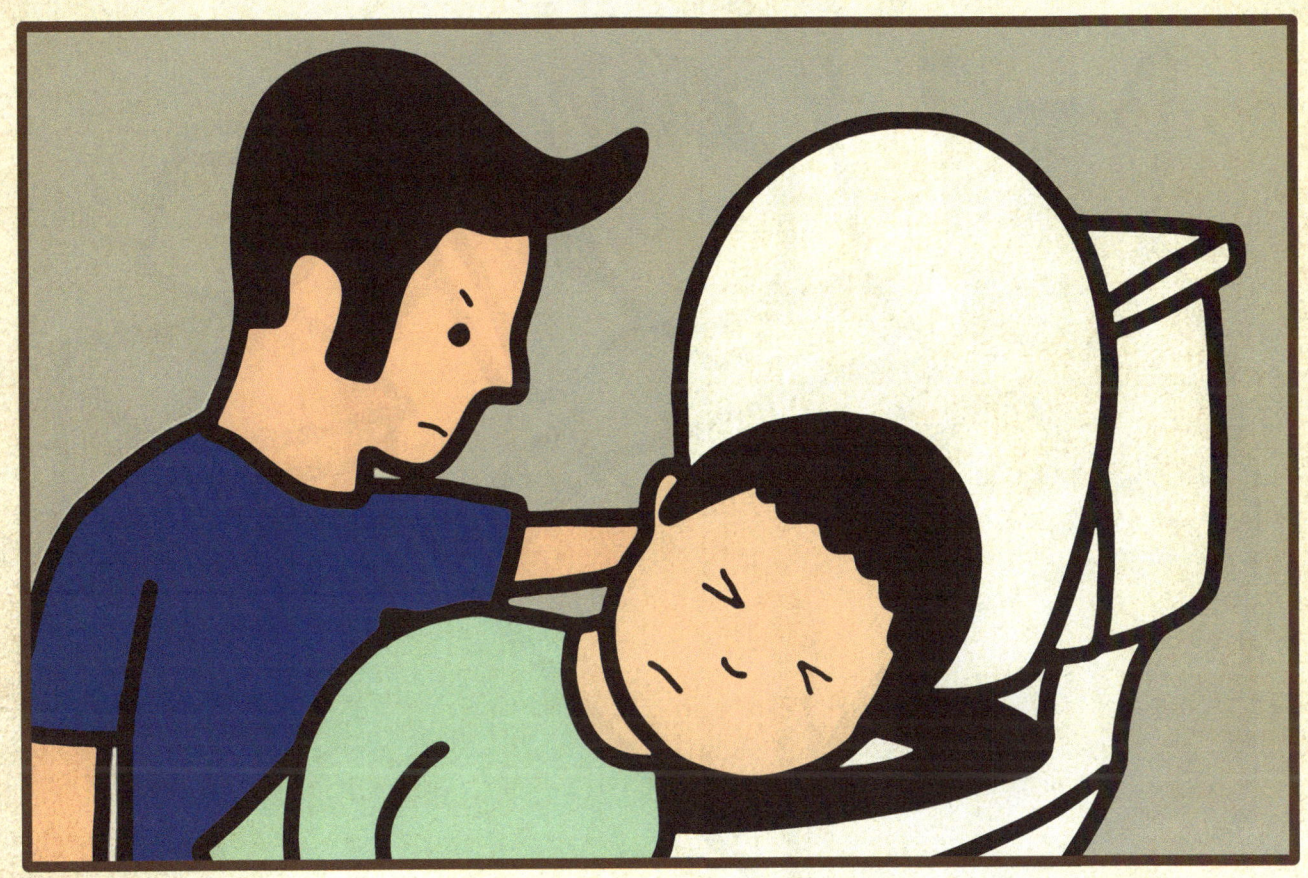

When Mom and Dad went on a rare date, Stephen would babysit me. These were always wild nights that included Stephen trying to flush my head down the toilet.

THE BOOMER ARCHAEOLOGIST
· CHAPTER 3 ·

By the time Mom and Dad returned home, I'd be exhausted and fast asleep. By the next morning, I'd forget whatever happened on the previous crazy evening. Only in the mid-2000s did I recall these events in therapy. ✺

Post-WWII California Dreamin'
1950s in the San Fernando Valley

Lily and Uncle Tom on Computer Video Call

LILY IN STREATHAM

Your family faced antisemitism in Europe, came to America and joined the working class. I've heard people talk about the "American Dream." Did that happen for your family?

UNCLE TOM IN BORREGO SPRINGS

Yes, both sides of my family wanted to be accepted as Americans. This meant assimilating and losing a lot of their European-Jewish culture. I feel sorry about this loss. They believed, as I do, that every person in the USA has an equal opportunity to prosper and succeed through hard work and innovation — the American Dream. As you saw in my father's story, this was worth fighting for in WWII and Korea. However, "success" can't be measured and it means different things in different contexts.

THE BOOMER ARCHAEOLOGIST

THOMAS EVAN LEVY

• CHAPTER 4 •

1960s

In the Valley

THE BOOMER ARCHAEOLOGIST
CHAPTER 4

In 1959, when I was 6 and my cousin Jeff was 7, we started selling newspapers every Sunday at St. Joseph the Worker Church in the San Fernando Valley. I "retired" as a paperboy in 1966, in time for my Bar Mitzvah.

Growing up, in 1957, my uncle Gene bought a piece of land in Wrightwood, California. Almost every weekend for 5 years, my dad, Uncle Gene, Uncle Jay, and Great Uncle Joe helped to build a family cabin. Jeff and I would accompany them and play while they worked.

1960s
In the Valley

THE BOOMER ARCHAEOLOGIST
• CHAPTER 4 •

On April 16, 1960, my grandpa Abe had a heart attack at his home in Reseda, California. Jeff and I were playing in the front yard when Dad and Uncle Jay carried Grandpa to the car to rush him to the hospital, where he died at the age of 69.

1960s
In the Valley

In 1963, at the age of 10, I started Hebrew School at Temple Judea, a Reform synagogue in the Valley. My parents were founding members of this synagogue, which had been established among dilapidated buildings in an abandoned orange grove. As a kid in the Hebrew school there, never having been to Israel, I imagined that the citrus grove and beat-up houses must have been exactly what Israel was like. My Hebrew teacher, Mrs. Brodsky, inspired my early love for Israel.

THE BOOMER ARCHAEOLOGIST
· CHAPTER 4 ·

MOM GRADUATES WITH A BA IN ENGLISH, JUNE 1966.

My mother had dropped out of Skidmore College in upstate New York when she married my father in 1946. Back then, it was against the rules for women, at this women's college, to marry. In 1965, with Dad's strong support, she resumed her studies at Valley State College (now California State University Northridge). My mom's anthropology professor, Council "Count" Taylor, became a dear family friend. From the age of 11, Count educated me to become an anthropologist. Count taught our family about the links between African, African-American, and Jewish struggles against oppression.

1960s
In the Valley

By May 1967, 8 months after my Bar Mitzvah, Egypt had expelled UN peacekeepers in the Sinai Desert bordering Israel; they had also blockaded the Straits of Tiran and Israel's access to their Red Sea port. Israel was scared and considered this as an act of war.

THE BOOMER ARCHAEOLOGIST
· CHAPTER 4 ·

Nasser's actions led to Israel's preemptive strike on Egypt and Syria on June 5. In 6 days, Israel miraculously conquered its enemies. Here, General Uzi Narkiss (left), Defense Minister Moshe Dayan (center), and Chief of Staff Yitzhak Rabin (right) are in the Old City of Jerusalem during the Six-Day War.

Since its founding in 1948, Israel has been threatened with annihilation by its Arab neighbors. In 1967, as a 14-year-old, Israel's stunning victory over the belligerent Arab armies in the Six-Day War enthralled and awakened in me a deep love for Zionism.

1960s
In the Valley

Lily and Uncle Tom on Phone Call

LILY IN LONDON

I was amazed to read how, when you were growing up, your family was so friendly with an African-American professor. I thought African-Americans and Jews didn't get along.

UNCLE TOM IN SAN DIEGO

During the 1960s, African-Americans were struggling for their civil rights and many African countries were gaining their independence. Oppressed for almost 2,000 years, Jews were finally flourishing in the USA, and their newly reborn country of Israel was becoming an inspiring model of a successful post-colonial state. In general, the people of the 2 countries identified with each other. For the greater good, we needed to bring our communities back into alignment.

THE BOOMER ARCHAEOLOGIST

THE BOOMER ARCHAEOLOGIST

CHAPTER 5

The Late 1960s

Discovering Anthropology

THE BOOMER ARCHAEOLOGIST
◦ CHAPTER 5 ◦

My parents became dear friends with Council "Count" Taylor, one of Mom's professors in the Department of Anthropology at San Fernando Valley State College.

As a carpenter, Dad pounded nails every day for a living. Leaving for work at 5 a.m. and arriving home by 4 p.m., he would relax with a beer, sitting on the kitchen floor. Seeing how hard my dad exerted his body for a living, I decided not to follow in his footsteps.

The Late 1960s
Discovering Anthropology

TOMMY LISTENING TO DISCUSSION ON ANTHROPOLOGY AND AFRICA

In 1964, Count started to visit our home regularly and became Dad's drinking buddy. I was then 11 years old, and Count would share stories about his research in Africa. I began to understand how anthropology, with its focus on non-industrial societies, provided a window on how to understand the human condition.

By the time I was 13, in 1966, Count had given me a number of books to read about anthropology. I loved Colin Turnbull's ethnography about the Mbuti Pygmies who lived in the Ituri Forest of Congo. I learned about the significance of rites of passage in their society and discussed it in my Bar Mitzvah speech in relation to my Torah portion.

The Bar Mitzvah boy, 1966
Temple Judea
San Fernando Valley

The Late 1960s
Discovering Anthropology

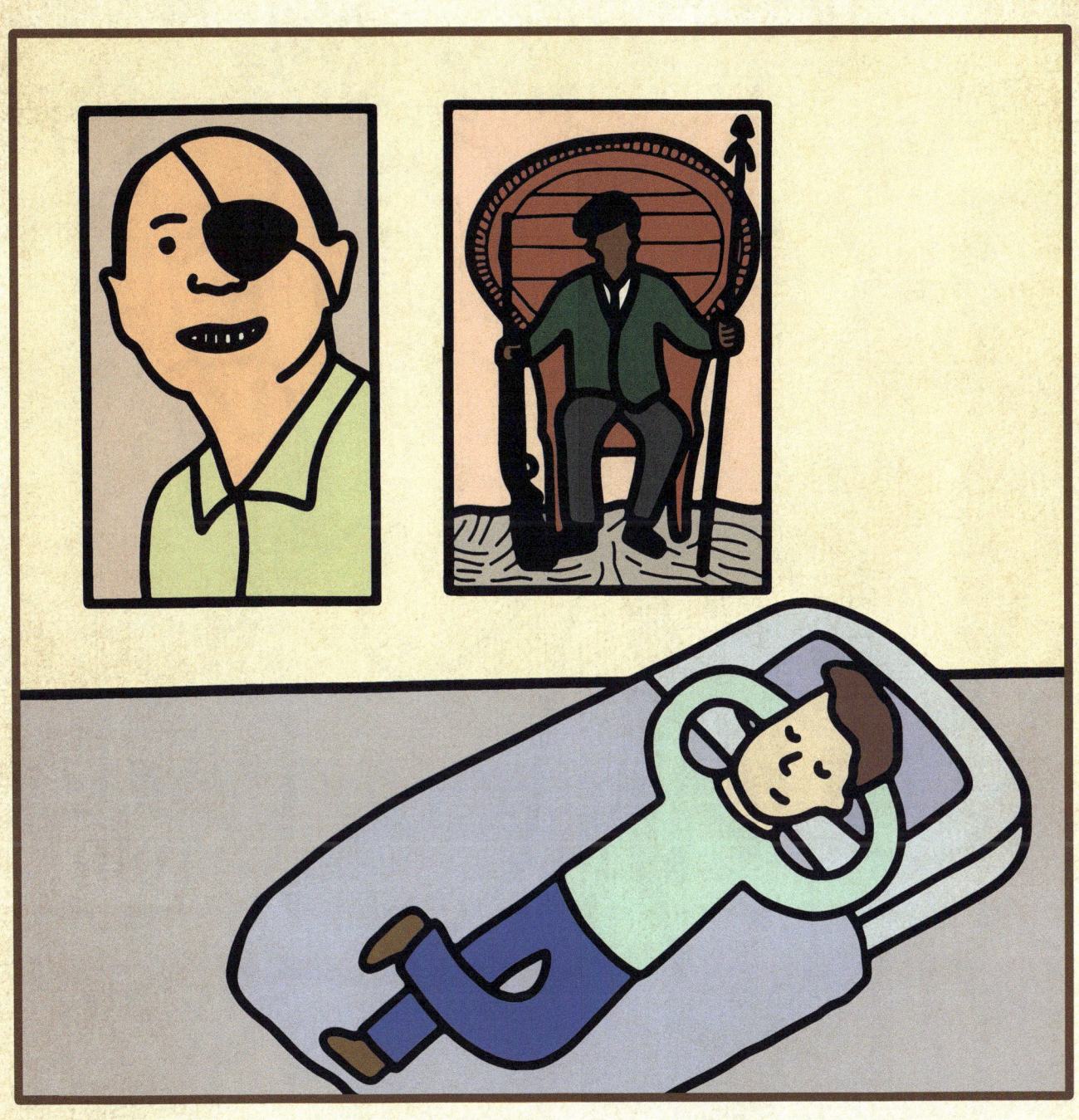

By 1967, my heroes were Israeli freedom fighters like General Moshe Dayan, Black Panther leader Huey Newton, and other revolutionaries whose posters adorned my room.

THE BOOMER ARCHAEOLOGIST
• CHAPTER 5 •

Count and his young Trinidadian roommate, Bob Reece, would host wild '60s parties at Count's home on Rayen Street. As a young teenager, I accompanied my parents to these happenings — getting an eyeful. My parents were more observers than participants in these parties. ✿

The Late 1960s
Discovering Anthropology

Lily and Uncle Tom on Phone Video Call

LILY'S LIVING ROOM IN LONDON

YOU WERE REALLY LUCKY TO MEET COUNT TAYLOR AS A KID AND TO HAVE EARLY ON DEVELOPED A LOVE FOR ANTHROPOLOGY. THE 1960s SEEM LIKE PRETTY WILD TIMES; WHY?

UNCLE TOM'S BACKYARD

AFTER WWII, AMERICA BECAME THE LEADING SUPERPOWER. INNOVATIONS IN SCIENCE, TECHNOLOGY, AND EDUCATION HAPPENED AT LIGHTNING SPEED. NEW INVENTIONS LIKE THE "PILL" RADICALLY CHANGED YOUNG AMERICANS' CONCEPTS OF TRADITIONAL MORALITY. UNLIKE WWII, AND THE KOREAN WAR, MANY AMERICANS COULD NOT SEE THE POINT OF FIGHTING A COMMON ENEMY LIKE THE FASCISTS AND COMMUNISTS OF EARLIER WARS. YOUNG PEOPLE REBELLED BY EMBRACING NEW ROCK AND ROLL MUSIC, NEW PSYCHEDELICS, AND OTHER DRUGS.

THE BOOMER ARCHAEOLOGIST

THOMAS EVAN LEVY

· CHAPTER 6 ·

Road to Anthropology

Late 1960s–1970

THE BOOMER ARCHAEOLOGIST
• CHAPTER 6 •

With a PhD from Yale, Council "Count" Taylor was a Black anthropologist and professor who worked in West Africa. As a friend of the Levy family, Count introduced us to Black Power; and me, as an 11-year-old, to anthropology. Count and my dad were drinking buddies and kindred spirits. One of his students said, "Malcolm went to jail, and Council went to Yale."

Road to Anthropology
Late 1960s-1970

By the age of 13, I realized I could not travel to Africa and be a cultural anthropologist like Count. In 1967, I volunteered on my first "dig" in the Pacific Palisades neighborhood of Los Angeles, and fell in love with archaeology.

In 1968, my best friend and cousin Jeff received a beautiful Ford Mustang convertible from his parents for his 16th birthday. I was 15.5 years old when we drove up to our family cabin in Wrightwood, California. The trip was gonna be sex, drugs, and rock and roll!

THE BOOMER ARCHAEOLOGIST
• CHAPTER 6 •

That night, Jeff and his girlfriend each took a "tab" of LSD, aka Acid. 3 tabs were placed on the living room table. When the moment came for me to "drop acid," I chickened out.

Jeff took my tab, and a few hours later, he was on a very bad trip. I spent the night in the cabin's tiny bathroom, "talking Jeff down" from the trip. After that experience, I decided never to experiment with hard drugs.

Road to Anthropology
Late 1960s-1970

My high school, James Monroe, was mostly attended by white kids. In the spring of 1968, a young black guy appeared on the football field, all alone. I invited him to sit with me. His name was David Ndegwa, and he was a member of the Kikuyu tribe — the same as Kenya's first president, Jomo Kenyatta. Count had given me Kenyatta's book "Facing Mount Kenya." Several months later, we invited David to live with us. He stayed for over 2 years as part of our family. ✿

CHAPTER 7

I Am a Jew

A Message to All Minorities, 1969–1971

THE BOOMER ARCHAEOLOGIST
• CHAPTER 7 •

David Ndegwa and I became close friends. His was like the Joseph story. The youngest son of one of his father's many wives, David was his dad's favorite. When David came to live in Los Angeles with his half-brother, the man took  all of David's money. Penniless and destitute, David came to live with us as my "brother." He called my dad "Mzee" — a title of respect for parents and elders in Swahili. The Levy's home for lost boys flourished.

The Negro Speaks of Rivers
By Langston Hughes

I've known rivers:
I've known rivers ancient as the world and older
than the flow of human blood in human veins.

My soul has grown deep like the rivers.

I bathed in the Euphrates when dawns were young.
I built my hut near the Congo and it lulled me to sleep.
I looked upon the Nile and raised the pyramids above it.
I heard the singing of the Mississippi when Abe Lincoln
went down to New Orleans, and I've seen its muddy
bosom turn all golden in the sunset.

I've known rivers:
Ancient, dusky rivers.

My soul has grown deep like the rivers.

THE BOOMER ARCHAEOLOGIST
▫ CHAPTER 7 ▫

Inspired by Langston Hughes, I tried my 16-year-old hand at poetry in 1969...

I am a Jew:
A Message to All Minorities

I'm a Jew and I really like it.
I never heard it said that way...
So I said it.

I'm sure a lot of us feel that way.
But why don't we say it?
We are not White.

And why do some of us pretend that we are?
And why do our friends think we are?

God damn it, I'm no Whiteman.
Don't tell me I am.
After slavery, the Inquisition,
and extermination...
You want to tell me I'm White?
I can't take that.

Know that I am a Jew.
Know that I too have feelings.
Know that I'm proud.

THE BOOMER ARCHAEOLOGIST
◦ CHAPTER 7 ◦

My uncle Steve, who had been a teenage troublemaker, metamorphized in 10 years into an awesome graduate student at the University of California, Los Angeles (UCLA); doing a PhD in History on the Jewish community in Weimar, Germany. Steve (now aka Stephen) and his wife Evie lived near campus, and with them I would often hang out and stay overnight. Seeing Stephen up at 6 a.m. surrounded by his books, banging away at the typewriter, listening to Mozart on the record player, and smoking German cigars was so cool. I could not wait to get to college.

I Am a Jew
A Message to All Minorities, 1969–1971

TOM IN FRONT OF JAMES MONROE HIGH SCHOOL

In 1970, Steve traveled with Evie to Berlin for his doctoral research. Steve would cross into East Berlin each day at Checkpoint Charlie, and make his way to the Jewish newspaper archives in the Staatsbibliothek. Before leaving for Germany, Steve lent me his 1964 Dodge Rambler. My high school buddies called me the Midnight Rambler. The car had a huge leak in the radiator, requiring a top-up every time I drove it. I had to keep 10 gallons of water on the back seat to keep the radiator going.

THE BOOMER ARCHAEOLOGIST
▫ CHAPTER 7 ▫

In June 1971, as a 17-year-old, I flew on an Icelandair Airline projet from New York City to join Steve and Evie in Berlin. This was my first trip to Europe, and I was on my way, alone, to Israel for the first time! For a month, I accompanied Steve on his research trips to East Berlin, and together with Evie, we visited the Dachau Concentration Camp, and Prague in Soviet-occupied Czechoslovakia. I did not know then that my father had helped liberate Dachau 26 years earlier. Why didn't Dad tell this to our family?

Prague would become very important in my life when, almost 50 years later, Charles University awarded me an honorary doctorate. ✪

I Am a Jew
A Message to All Minorities, 1969–1971

Lily and Uncle Tom on Computer Video Call

SPRING IN LONDON

YOU WERE REMARKABLY INDEPENDENT AT 17 YEARS OF AGE. WHAT HAPPENED TO YOUR FRIEND DAVID NDEGWA WHEN YOU LEFT HOME FOR ISRAEL?

STRONG WINDS IN SAN DIEGO

IN A NUTSHELL, AFTER I LEFT FOR ISRAEL, DAVID SUFFERED FROM "CULTURE-SHOCK." MY FATHER AND COUNT WERE HAVING A DRINK ONE AFTERNOON IN OUR KITCHEN. COUNT WAS SURPRISED WHEN MY FATHER SERVED HIM A WATERED-DOWN RUM. IT SOON BECAME CLEAR THAT DAVID HAD DEVELOPED A DRINKING PROBLEM AS HE WAS REFILLING DAD'S LIQUOR BOTTLES WITH WATER AND NEGLECTING HIS COLLEGE STUDIES. DAVID GOT IN TROUBLE WITH THE POLICE, WAS IMPRISONED, AND MONTHS LATER THE KENYAN EMBASSY HAD DAVID RETURNED TO KENYA, WHERE DAVID WENT ON A DOWNWARD SPIRAL. IT WAS VERY SAD.

THE BOOMER ARCHAEOLOGIST

CHAPTER 8

Journey to the Holy Land

Archaeology and Kibbutz, 1971

THE BOOMER ARCHAEOLOGIST
• CHAPTER 8 •

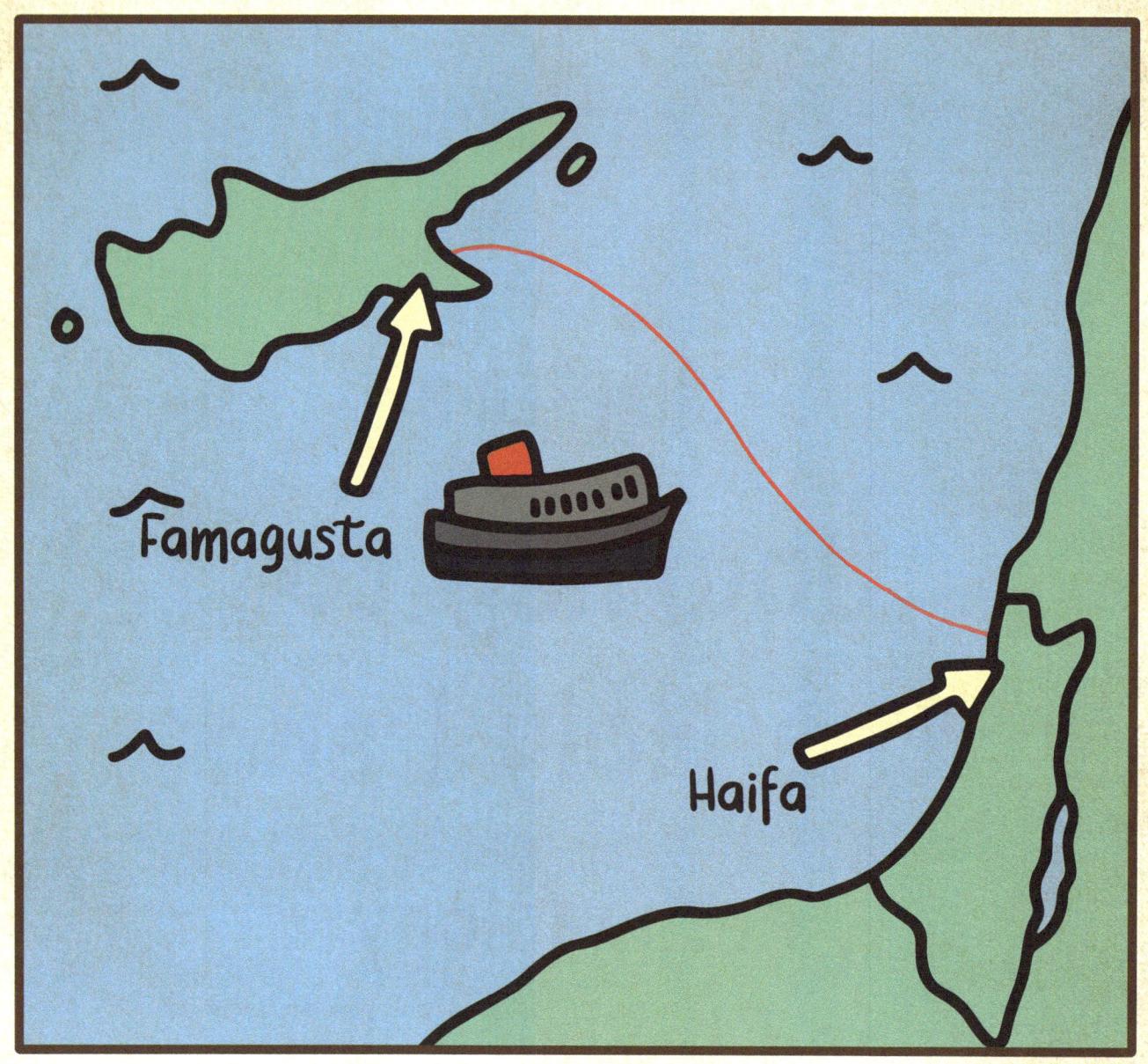

Before "Birthright" and organized youth-group tours, as a 17-year-old, I made my way to Israel alone, flying from East Berlin to the Island of Cyprus. The heat and blaring cicadas welcomed me to the east. Traveling on the overnight ferry from Famagusta, I arrived in Haifa.

Journey to the Holy Land
Archaeology and Kibbutz, 1971

Making my way to Jerusalem, I slept on the roof of a Yeshiva in the Old City. Eventually, a beat-up Egged bus took me to the Hebrew Union College excavations at Tel Gezer, where I quickly became assistant photographer — and accidently tripped, breaking the project's very expensive Hasselblad camera. I only told the dig director, Professor Dever, about this accident about 35 years later, when he spoke at my endowed chair ceremony in San Diego.

THE BOOMER ARCHAEOLOGIST
• CHAPTER 8 •

The Gezer excavations were one of the first interdisciplinary archaeology expeditions in the Levant; they used state-of-the-art techniques like an on-site air-conditioned dark room to develop and print photos the same day. As assistant photographer, I got to see all the excavation areas being revealed each day by the +130 member team. Developing film and printing photos daily was literally so cool.

Journey to the Holy Land
Archaeology and Kibbutz, 1971

Growing up in a lower-middle-class family, I was anxious to experience the pure socialism of the kibbutz. After the Gezer dig, I volunteered for 6 months at Kibbutz Ashdot Ya'akov Meuhad in the Jordan Valley, starting in the Banana fields but enthusiastically becoming a cowboy in the dairy. After several months, the kibbutz chose me to represent the volunteers at a week-long seminar at the kibbutz headquarters in Tel Aviv. There, I enthusiastically embraced the socialist propaganda we were fed. I also found my first girlfriend, whose last name was also "Levy."

THE BOOMER ARCHAEOLOGIST
◦ CHAPTER 8 ◦

At Gezer, I became good friends with the Tanour family, the expedition cooks from the Palestinian city of Nablus (Biblical Shechem). I spent 2 nights as their house guest, feasting, watching Indian films at the city cinema, and eating street food. I contracted high-risk hepatitis.

Journey to the Holy Land
Archaeology and Kibbutz, 1971

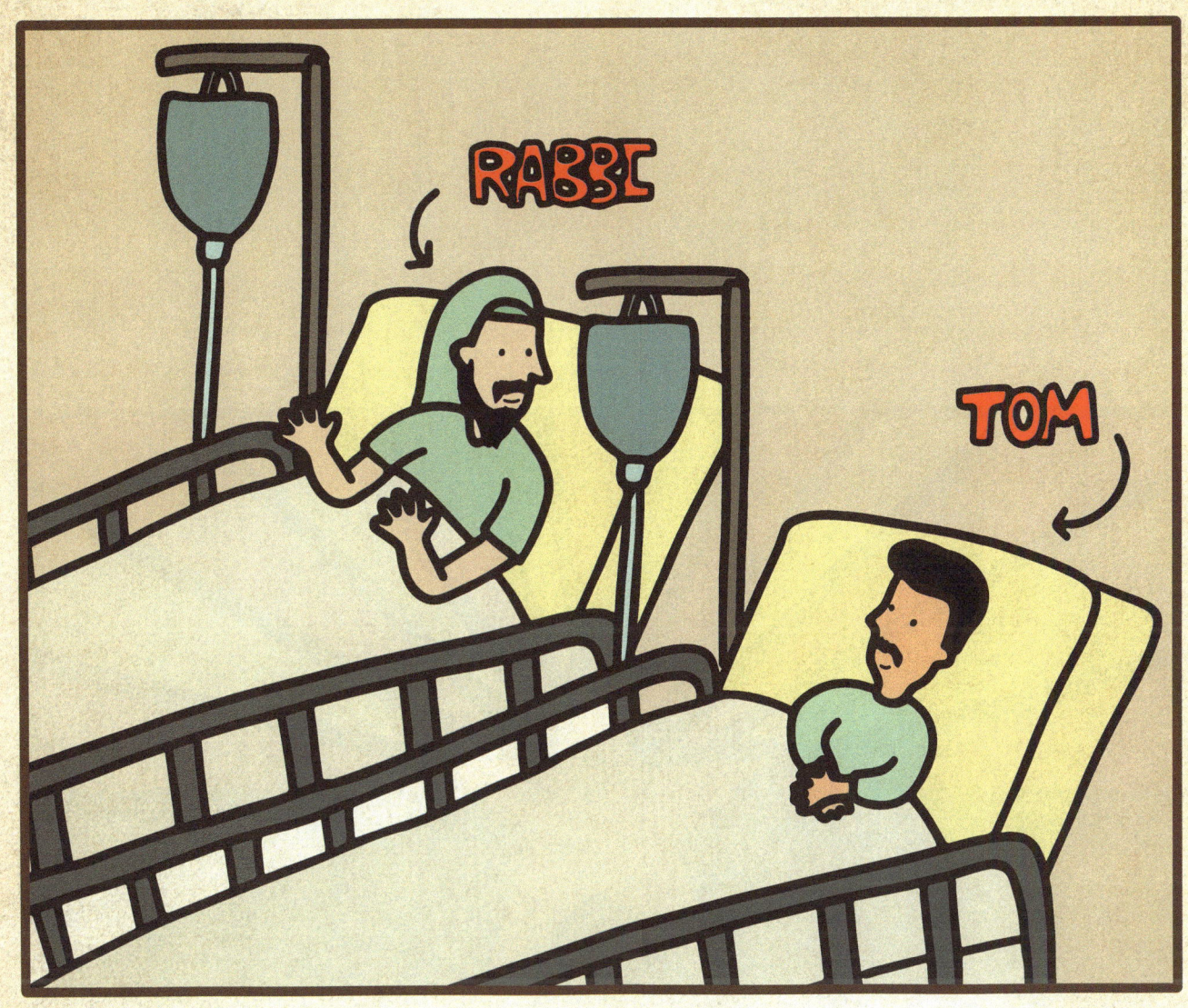

The day after I returned to the kibbutz in late November 1971, my Ulpan teacher took one look at my yellow eyes and called an ambulance. At Poriyah Hospital, overlooking the Sea of Galilee, my roommate for the week was an elderly Moroccan Tzadik — a Rabbi and a mystic. At that time, my Hebrew was not so great. I could not understand most of what the Rabbi said; however, he radiated love and created in me a sense of belonging with the Jewish people.

CHAPTER 9

To the Old Pueblo

Discovering Behavioral Archaeology, 1973

THE BOOMER ARCHAEOLOGIST
• CHAPTER 9 •

From 1969, I was part of Jack Zahniser's UCLA spring expeditions to Hohokam sites around the Rincon Valley near Tucson. There I met Gary Stickel, one of Jack's fellow grad students. By 1972, as a pretty good cartographer, I was helping Gary (who had just earned his PhD) with a National Science Foundation (NSF) grant proposal he was preparing for the famous UCLA archaeologist, Marija Gimbutas. My job would involve making all the proposal maps for a cool Neolithic project in Northern Greece. If they got the grant, I would be a part of the expedition.

To the Old Pueblo
Discovering Behavioral Archaeology, 1973

In 1970, I attended Jack's field school near Taos, New Mexico. A Native American kid from the pueblo told me, "Tom, this is not your archaeology. You should work on your own culture." That convinced me to focus on the Mediterranean world.

In September 1972, at the age of 18, I was working as a student with the archaeology unit at San Fernando Valley State College. On September 5, 1972, Palestinian terrorists stormed the Olympic Village in Munich, Germany, which ended with the massacre of 11 Israelis — 5 athletes and 6 other members of the Olympic team. I was mortified when my American student colleagues said the Israeli sportsmen "got what they deserved."

THE BOOMER ARCHAEOLOGIST
· CHAPTER 9 ·

Disgusted with my fellow Southern California (SoCal) students, I applied to the University of Arizona (U of A) and got out of Los Angeles within 4 months of being accepted for BA studies in anthropology. My dad lent me his old Dodge van, and in January 1973, I drove out to Tucson.

To the Old Pueblo
Discovering Behavioral Archaeology, 1973

There were exceptional archaeology professors at the U of A. I was closest to Norman Yoffee, William Dever (who had just arrived from Israel, where he directed the dig at Gezer!), and the 27-year-old powerhouse, Michael Schiffer, who was creating a new subfield called "Behavioral Archaeology." I'm still in touch with these "giants."

THE BOOMER ARCHAEOLOGIST
◦ CHAPTER 9 ◦

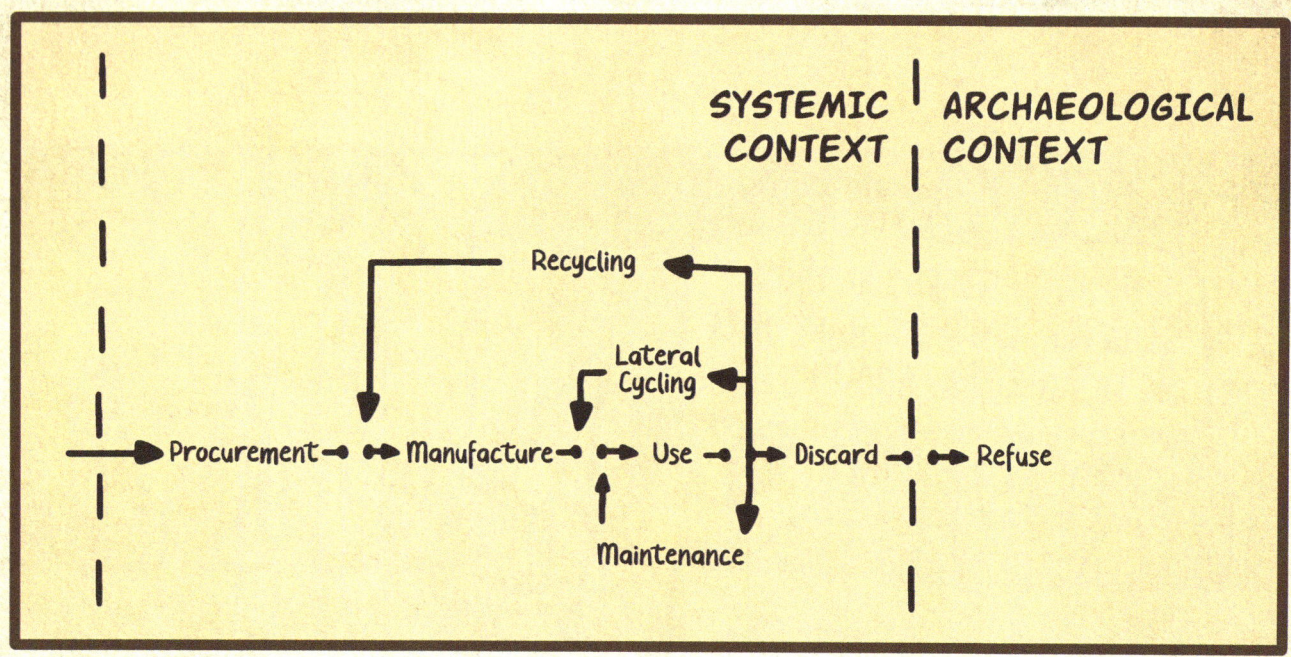

According to Schiffer's new Behavioral Archaeology paradigm, all behavior (defined as activities) consists of people-artifact interactions. He also promoted the importance of natural and cultural formation processes to understand how the archaeological record was formed. I drew many of the diagrams for his first book. To this day, Behavioral Archaeology underpins a lot of my research and professional writing.

One of the beauties of Behavioral Archaeology is that it enables us to go from the static archaeological record we excavate to the dynamic cultures that actually lived at these sites. In this sense, we go from the archaeological context to the context of the living cultural system that produced it, as shown in the diagram above.

To the Old Pueblo
Discovering Behavioral Archaeology, 1973

Lily and Uncle Tom on Email

A "HURLY-BURLY" IN LONDON

I READ SOMEWHERE THAT SOME AMERICAN ARCHAEOLOGISTS IN THE 1950s SAID "ARCHAEOLOGY IS ANTHROPOLOGY OR IT IS NOTHING." DO YOU BELIEVE THAT?

HOT AND DRY IN BORREGO SPRINGS

AS AN UNDERGRADUATE AT THE U OF A IN THE EARLY 1970s, YES I DID. BACK THEN, THE ANTHROPOLOGICAL APPROACH EMPHASIZED THE STUDY OF SOCIAL EVOLUTION IN DEEP TIME. ANTHROPOLOGICAL MODELS HELP US UNDERSTAND HOW SOCIETIES GROW, STABILIZE, AND COLLAPSE. HOWEVER, ANTHROPOLOGY TODAY IS MORE INTERESTED IN CURRENT POLITICS AND POWER THAN IN STUDYING TRADITIONAL SOCIETIES. TODAY, I THINK ARCHAEOLOGY AT US UNIVERSITIES SHOULD BE A SEPARATE FIELD, DIVORCED FROM ANTHROPOLOGY, WHICH HAS BECOME THE SAME AS SOCIOLOGY AND ETHNIC STUDIES.

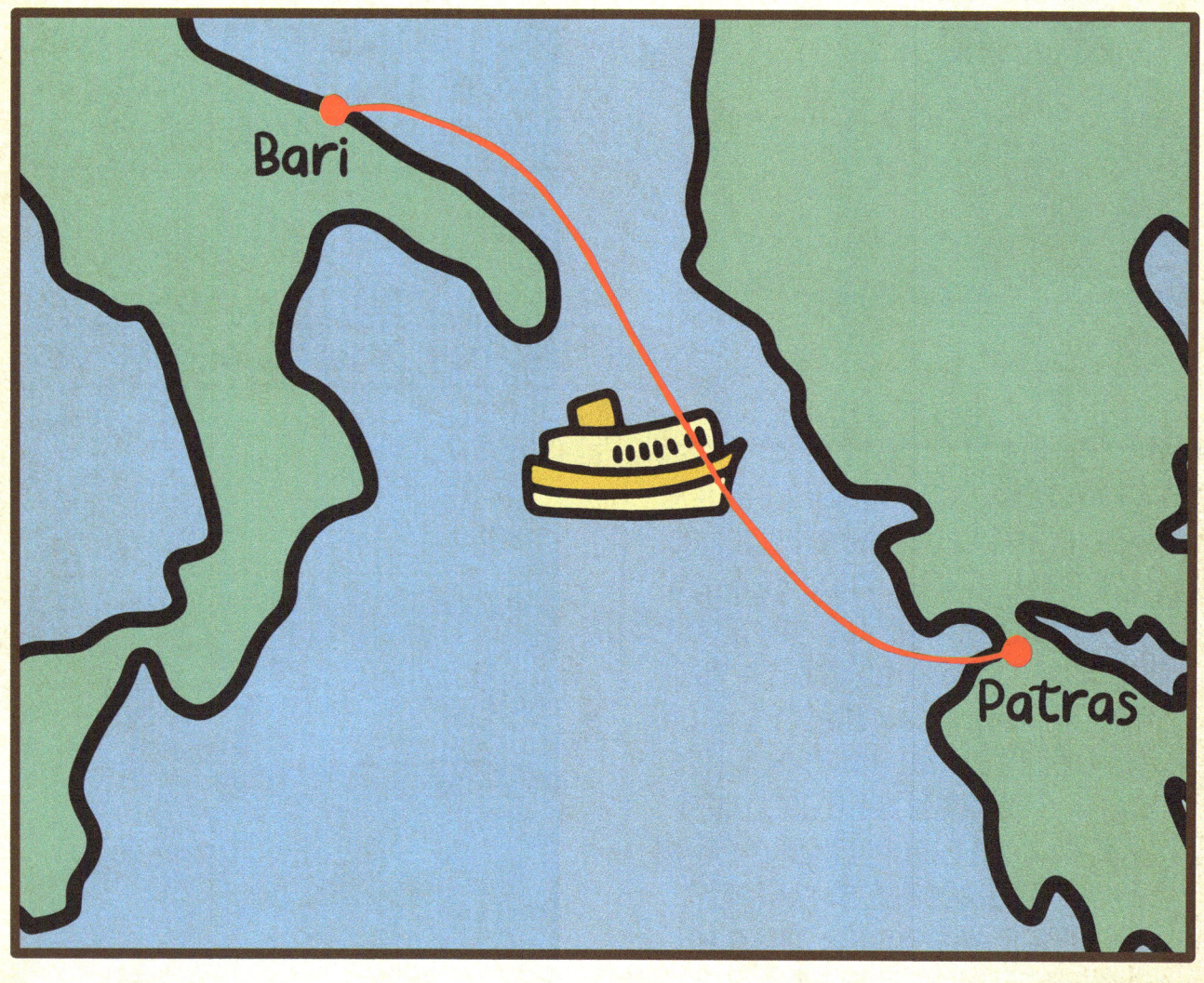

CHAPTER 10

Sailing the Wine-Dark Sea

Greece, 1973

THE BOOMER ARCHAEOLOGIST
CHAPTER 10

In 1973, the NSF proposal was funded! Our expedition to Greece began by picking up a brand-new Fiat Station Wagon in Torino, Italy, and taking the ferry from Bari to Patras, Greece. I was assigned to be the expedition driver. On arrival, we were detained by customs when they found 2 walkie-talkies in my luggage. These were considered espionage tools and so were stamped in my passport. I could not leave Greece without them in hand.

Sailing the Wine-Dark Sea
Greece, 1973

We left the car in Volos and sailed to Alonnisos to explore Neolithic sites on the Northern Sporades islands. On arrival, we rented a small caïque to survey around the islands. The next morning, as we loaded onto the boat, 2 beautiful Greek women unexpectedly joined our group. The fisherman was making some extra money. Bruce Butzbach — a UCLA grad student on our project, a local Greek muscleman, and I were happy to welcome our unexpected guests aboard.

THE BOOMER ARCHAEOLOGIST
• CHAPTER 10 •

In Volos, we met Professor Dimitris Theocharis, the Greek co-principal investigator of our project. He urged us to sail to the tiny 5th millennium BC Neolithic island called Agios Petros, which he had sampled. The minute we approached it, I fell in love with the site. After a long day, we sailed back to the island of Alonnisos — our base.

Sailing the Wine-Dark Sea
Greece, 1973

To prepare for my first trip to Greece, I had carefully studied Nikos Kazantzakis' book, "Zorba the Greek," and kept a keen eye out for widows. To my surprise, when we got off the boat, our fellow travelers, Artemis and Arete, invited me to join them for a late-night dinner at the seaside taverna. I was intrigued by these women. In Greek mythology, Artemis was the goddess of the hunt and Arete, the goddess of virtue and goodness. Artemis was around 40 (about 21 years older than me), and Arete was 27 (8 years older than me).

THE BOOMER ARCHAEOLOGIST
• CHAPTER 10 •

After having a lot of ouzo, octopus, and olives, Artemis, who spoke excellent English, said that she and Arete would like to invite me to go swimming with them. When I said my bathing suit was up the hill at my hotel, she said that I would not need it.

Sailing the Wine-Dark Sea
Greece, 1973

When Arete got out of the water, she looked like one of those spectacular statues of Aphrodite found in Cyprus. To my surprise, Arete invited me to her room. I thought of Kazantzakis who said, "Happy is the man, I thought, who, before dying, has the good fortune to sail the Aegean sea." Arete became my girlfriend for the rest of my time in Greece. Doing archaeology in Greece was looking better by the minute. ✦

• CHAPTER 11 •
Yom Kippur War, 1973

THE BOOMER ARCHAEOLOGIST
▫ CHAPTER 11 ▫

Our excavation took place at a small prehistoric settlement on the Plain of Thessaly in Northern Greece. Professor Marija Gimbutas was developing an intriguing theory about the Neolithic-European Mother Goddess. However, on the Achilleion dig, she showed little respect to her Greek partner, Professor Theocharis. Strangely, Gimbutas ignored the Greek half of the excavation.

Yom Kippur War, 1973

Achilleion was an amazing site that shed light on the expansion of Neolithic agriculture into Europe. My jobs were surveyor and photographer. A tall order for a 19-year-old, but I made the topographic map of the site and photographed many remarkable anthropomorphic figurines that were eventually published.

THE BOOMER ARCHAEOLOGIST
CHAPTER 11

According to the NSF proposal, at the end of the project, Professor Gimbutas was supposed to pay me $600. Marija refused and said that she would only give me $60. We argued, and it was clear that Marija was an antisemite when she said, "You people are only concerned with money."

Yom Kippur War, 1973

Marija said that if I wanted more money, I would have to stay in the village on my own for 2 weeks and do extra work. I was handed $200, the team left, and I stayed on. By early September, I went to Athens to study Modern Greek. The only place I could afford to rent was in a slum at the base of Mount Lykavitos. I dined with Arete and friends, but often ate alone, subsisting on plain spaghetti at a neighborhood restaurant. The waiters were kind and often gave me free bread and olives.

THE BOOMER ARCHAEOLOGIST
CHAPTER 11

The Yom Kippur War broke out in October 1973. As broadcast on the radio, country after country abandoned Israel in the wake of the surprise attack on Jews' most holy day — Yom Kippur, the Day of Atonement. I was determined to volunteer in Israel. Thus, began an intense correspondence with Marija, who was on a sabbatical in Europe, to make an affidavit that the walkie-talkies listed in my passport were in her possession. Once this was finally cleared, I said goodbye to Arete and flew to Israel.

Yom Kippur War, 1973

I arrived by mid-October at Lod Airport (now Ben Gurion International Airport) in Israel, to an eerie blacked-out Tel Aviv. The receptionist at the volunteer desk asked me what I could do to help. I proudly said, "Milk cows," and she handed me a bus ticket to Kibbutz Eilot in the Arava Valley, near Eilat. David Ben-Gurion, the founding prime minister of Israel, passed away on December 1. I spent those months quite pleased, working again in the cowshed, helping my fellow Jews at a very difficult time; this was when the state of Israel was only 25 years old, and most people thought it might be annihilated. After a disastrous beginning, Israel prevailed, and a ceasefire went into effect on October 24, 1973. By mid-December, I was back in Tucson. ✡

THE BOOMER ARCHAEOLOGIST

CHAPTER 12

Back to Tucson and Back to Home, 1974

THE BOOMER ARCHAEOLOGIST
• CHAPTER 12 •

The drive back to Tucson was slow in my 1959 Chevy Apache. I was 20 years old, and it gave me time to think about the experiences of Greece and war-torn Israel. By the time I got to our house at 731 E 4th Street, just down the road from the old Geronimo Hotel, my roommate Mike Rigby was sitting on the front porch. After a beer, I proclaimed my decision to do my PhD fieldwork at Agios Petros, the small Neolithic island in Greece.

Back to Tucson and Back to Home, 1974

The house we rented was built in the 1920s, near the Department of Anthropology. It was owned by a Jewish guy, Harry, who was in his early 40s. Harry made a decent income from his rentals, and spent most warm days naked in the backyard, smoking pot. Mike and I studied on the back porch. One day, Harry introduced us to our neighbor Alice and her little 7-year-old boy.

THE BOOMER ARCHAEOLOGIST
• CHAPTER 12 •

Some days later, Alice invited me over for dinner at her massive old house. The adjoining rickety backyard fence made an easy passage to her place from ours. Watercolors were her passion, and she was a gifted artist. In no time, Alice evolved into Al. At 36, Al was 16 years older than me. Al the artist would spend her evenings painting; and she was intrigued by my passion for black-and-white photography (using the Zone System). After several visits, Al invited me to spend the night with her. I quickly became infatuated with her, and trouble began looming...

Back to Tucson and Back to Home, 1974

I was keeping up with my studies but getting entangled in a months-long relationship that was going nowhere, fast. Finally, one summer night after a road trip to Los Angeles, Al said, "Thomas, you keep coming over here like a little puppy dog. Time for you to get out." I was heartbroken and had to go home for a semester to lick my emotional wounds. My parents and friends helped nurture me back from depression. Al had actually done me a great favor by kicking me out. ✦

THE BOOMER ARCHAEOLOGIST

CHAPTER 13

Licking My Wounds in the Valley, 1974

THE BOOMER ARCHAEOLOGIST
◦ CHAPTER 13 ◦

I withdrew from the U of A for a semester to lick my wounds from Alice's rejection, and stayed at my home in the San Fernando Valley. The warmth of my family and friends was awesome. I was able to spend a lot of time with my father — rebuilding a 1968 Triumph TR4 sports car, drinking Dos Equis beer, and talking. This was fortuitous because Dad would be dead 4 years later.

Licking My Wounds in the Valley, 1974

Dad was an avid hunter who enjoyed guns as a hobby, and firmly believed that Jews must be armed for self-defense. From the time I was a boy, we would go hunting and target shooting. Now that I was home again, we went shooting in the wilds at San Francisquito Canyon, north of Los Angeles, using our empty Dos Equis bottles for target practice. Just north of the Valley, the canyon attracted Black Panthers, Chicanos, White guys, and other armed groups. The hill slopes of the canyon glistened with broken bottles and brass shell casings. We were the only Jews out there.

THE BOOMER ARCHAEOLOGIST
▪ CHAPTER 13 ▪

In 1969, I started private Arabic lessons with Jim Waldron, an amazing man who could speak numerous dialects of Arabic. After returning to Los Angeles, Jim invited me to join Almas, his Arabic Folk Ensemble. We performed at Zorba's — a nightclub in the Valley. Jim could do an amazing Saudi sword dance, and we were his backup. My high school buddy, Robert Portillo, was part of the group. Jim was a cultural bridge-builder who had graduated from the Army Intelligence Language School in Monterey, California. Unfortunately, he died of HIV/AIDS in the early 80s.

Licking My Wounds in the Valley, 1974

One day, out of the blue, a card arrived from Charlene, a young woman who was a volunteer at Kibbutz Ashdot Ya'akov when I was there in 1971. She was such a positive person. Charlene invited me for dinner at her cool apartment in Marina del Rey — over the hill from our home in the San Fernando Valley. She asked me to stay with her overnight. After a month, Charlene suggested that I meet her next-door neighbor Susan and get to know her. Those women were independent, adventurous, and nurturing; they helped me through that troubled time. When Leonard Cohen talked about the "Great Truce," I think he meant Great Truce with North American women.

THE BOOMER ARCHAEOLOGIST
• CHAPTER 13 •

Another "therapy" at home was dreaming about working in Greece. Although I first qualified as a diver in 1969, I decided to requalify. The final dives were off the coast of Catalina Island in one of the submerged, beautiful kelp forests.

Licking My Wounds in the Valley, 1974

After 3 months in Los Angeles, I was good. Hanging out with my parents, especially my father and friends, was the perfect tonic for getting my confidence back. In the heat of an August morning in 1974, I said goodbye to Mom and Dad, fired up the TR4, and drove east to Tucson with my buddy, Tom Ludovise. I didn't have a canvas top for the Triumph, so it was an exceptionally hot 120°F drive through the desert. ✺

THE BOOMER ARCHAEOLOGIST

CHAPTER 14

The Road to Prehistory — Final U of A Days, 1975

THE BOOMER ARCHAEOLOGIST
• CHAPTER 14 •

I returned to Tucson, invigorated, and ready to finish my BA studies. It felt great to be back, living with my rommate, Mike Rigby, and studying hard at the university. I assumed Alice was still living behind our house, but I never saw her again.

I made a new friend — David Greenbaum, from the small town of Safford, Arizona. They were the only Jewish family in town, and so they invited me to spend a weekend with them. We took our guns out of Safford for target practice in the high desert.

The Road to Prehistory — Final U of A days, 1975

THE BOOMER ARCHAEOLOGIST
• CHAPTER 14 •

Most of the professors I studied closely with at the U of A were quite young. Along with Schiffer, there was Norman Yoffee, who let me take his graduate seminar in Mesopotamian archaeology. Norm was around 30 years old. At the time, there were no textbooks on this subject, so we created one under Norm's guidance — from prehistory to the 1st millennium BCE. I started taking his graduate course in Akkadian, but dropped out as you had to know German to translate the ancient texts. Only after earning the PhD did I call him "Norm."

The Road to Prehistory — Final U of A days, 1975

During my last semester at the U of A in 1975, William G. Dever, the noted Biblical archaeologist, got a job in the Near Eastern Studies Department. Dever had directed the Gezer excavation in which I participated 4 years earlier. He began teaching what he called "Syro-Palestinian" rather than "Biblical Archaeology." Today, most scholars call it "Levantine Archaeology," which is a less polarizing term. Dever arrived in Tucson with his wife Norma and son, Sean. Bill Dever, as his friends called him, was an awesome lecturer and teacher. I never called him "Bill" until after I earned my PhD.

THE BOOMER ARCHAEOLOGIST
• CHAPTER 14 •

That same semester, I took an Old World Prehistory course with Professor Arthur Jelinek — who some years earlier re-excavated the famous Tabun Cave site in Israel. The prominent French prehistorian, François Bordes, was his buddy, and so was spending a sabbatical in Tucson. When Bordes asked our class if anyone wanted to join his dig at the Neanderthal Cave site of Pech de l'Azé IV in Southwest France, I jumped at the opportunity. Bordes was active in the French underground in World War II. He loved America, was appreciative of what we did to help liberate Europe, and always wore a cowboy hat and bolo tie. Bordes highly respected my father as a fighter against the Germans.

We camped in the garden of Monsieur and Madame Denise de Sonneville-Bordes' lovely medieval farmhouse in the village of

The Road to Prehistory — Final U of A days, 1975

Carsac — not far from the cave. It was July and I was on my way to Sheffield to begin my doctoral studies in prehistory and archaeology. Before the dig, Bordes invited me to spend a month in his lab at the University of Bordeaux, learning Lithic Analysis. At the time, Bordes was the master of stone tool studies, and many prominent archaeologists studied under him. After excavating a 1 x 1 m grid square for a month with dental tools, paint brushes, and having to record the angle of every flake we found — I knew early prehistory was not for me. However, the 24/7 food and wine were wonderful. ✿

THOMAS EVAN LEVY

· CHAPTER 15 ·

The Full Monty — Early Days in Sheffield, 1976–1977

THE BOOMER ARCHAEOLOGIST
◦ CHAPTER 15 ◦

I chose the University of Sheffield because of their excellence in "Economic Prehistory" — a new paradigm developed by Eric Higgs from Cambridge. Some of Higgs' students, Robin Dennell and Graeme Barker, were young professors at Sheffield. As "Higglets," they led a new generation of researchers in method and theory. Robin became my supervisor, and Graeme, my unofficial advisor. The first day we met, Robin invited me to a local pub on Glossop Road near the department. Being an American, after 2 pints of bitter, I hardly remembered the library tour he gave me.

The Full Monty — Early Days in Sheffield, 1976–1977

At 23 years of age, the British system expected me to complete the PhD in 3 years. There were no required classes, and I still think that is ideal for graduate studies. The university computer center was down the street from our offices, so I wrote a Fortran program to create a 3D model of Agios Petros — the Neolithic island I fell in love with in 1973. This involved hanging out at the center and preparing paper punch cards to make a "deck" that was fed into a state-of-the-art IBM computer by a keypunch operator. The next day I would walk over to the center to obtain my results. This was all before the powers of personal computing. I spent my first year in Sheffield preparing to go to Greece for my fieldwork.

I had brought my Yves Saint Laurent suit with me to England, thinking it was a necessary attire to adapt to the university life in Britain. How wrong I was! My first roommate was Charlie, a medical student from Northern Ireland, who refused to say if he was a Catholic or Protestant. We lived in a row house on Stanfield Terrace. Charlie introduced me to Morris dancing, a

The Full Monty — Early Days in Sheffield, 1976–1977

type of English folk dance where men wear bells on their shins and wield sticks, swords, and handkerchiefs to the rhythmic music. I was part of the dance group for around 3 months. In retrospect, Charlie must have been a Protestant.

The Sheffield Lane Working Men's Club was not far from our flat. Charlie introduced me to it. The club was established in the 19th century to provide recreation and education for working-class men and their families. However, it wasn't until 2007 that women gained equal membership in this and other men's clubs around England. Back in 1976, the steel industry was still active in Sheffield but about to collapse. On Sundays, while the wives were at home cooking Sunday lunch, the men enjoyed strippers and a 2-piece band.

THE BOOMER ARCHAEOLOGIST
• CHAPTER 15 •

In March 1977, Ruth Goldstein, an undergraduate in my department and one of the few Jewish students I had met, invited me to a Hillel House event. With free falafel and Jaffa oranges, how could a struggling student refuse? Sitting on a sofa was the most beautiful woman I had ever seen. With her long dark hair, brown eyes, and beautiful lips, she was a consummate reflection of Sephardic beauty. I mustered up the courage to ask her in Hebrew, if she spoke Hebrew. She looked at me strangely and said in a British East African English accent, "What?" That was the first time I met Alina, and on the spot, I fell in love with her.

The Full Monty — Early Days in Sheffield, 1976–1977

I had spent the year preparing to do my fieldwork on Agios Petros in Greece. Professor Theocharis had arranged everything, and I was to work with his blessing and support. In mid-December, I received a letter from my good friend and Theocharis' nephew, George Papastamapolos, informing me that his dear uncle had unexpectedly passed away on December 2, 1977. The professor was only 58 years old, and not long before his death, he had completed "Neolithic Greece" — a beautiful large-format book published by the National Bank of Greece. I was shattered by this news, as all my plans to work in Greece suddenly went up in smoke. What could I possibly do to carry on with my PhD research? ✽

THE BOOMER ARCHAEOLOGIST

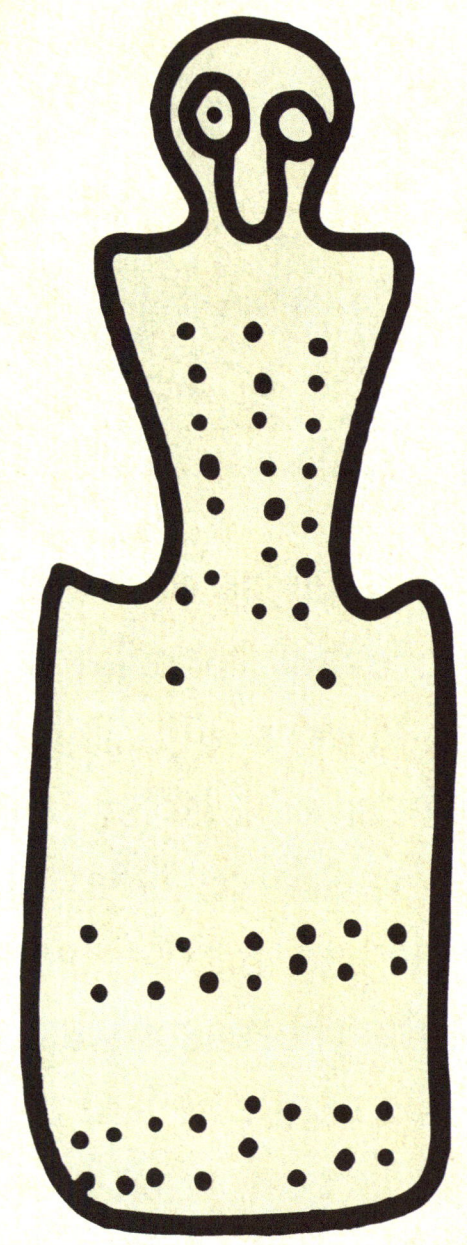

THOMAS EVAN LEVY

• CHAPTER 16 •

Back to the Holy Land, 1977

THE BOOMER ARCHAEOLOGIST
• CHAPTER 16 •

I was a poor student, and my accommodation in Sheffield reflected this. The row houses in Ruth Square, south of the university, had been spared during the WWII German bombings. The university owned a number of those flats, and I was fortunate to share one with Richard, an advanced student of architecture. Every night I could hear the next-door neighbor shouting and beating his wife. It was a depressing scene. In the morning, the old man would greet me at the back of the flat on our way to the outdoor loo, as if all was well. This was on the eve of receiving George's letter, and I was close to having Alina as my girlfriend.

Back to the Holy Land, 1977

After the free Jaffa oranges at Hillel, I bumped into Alina in the book stacks located in the bowels of the University of Sheffield library. It was a wonderful place to study, and Alina was at home down there studying for her final BSc exams in microbiology. We talked, she invited me to play squash (a game I never heard of), and after several weeks, I invited her to my place in Ruth Square for Bazella — an Arabic dish Jim Waldron taught me to cook with peas. To this day, Alina marvels that I had the chutzpah to make rice for an Indian woman.

I was shattered after learning that Professor Theocharis had died, and I immediately saw my dreams of working in Greece evaporate. Another bout of depression was sinking in, and I went to student health, where the doctor prescribed me some antidepressants. When Alina visited me in Ruth

THE BOOMER ARCHAEOLOGIST
· CHAPTER 16 ·

Square and saw the pills on the table, she said, "Pull your socks up and find somewhere else to work; and get rid of those pills! You will be fine. I'm here when you need me."

Sheffield was an awesome research environment. It was the real deal — the professors were encouraging, but graduate students had to find their own opportunities and funding. When things fell apart for me in Greece, I went to Dr. Graeme Barker's office and he said, "Tom, you worked

Back to the Holy Land, 1977

on a dig in Israel back in 1971, why don't you go back there and find a PhD project?" I moved into the Broom Hall Council Flats, a post-war derelict concrete complex where a classmate, Dave Fine, owned a flat. Dave rented out cheap space to me and Chris Gosden, who went on to become a renowned professor in archaeology at the University of Oxford. The 3 of us had fun. However, many of the residents were unemployed, depressed women who occasionally threw themselves off the upper floors, and on the way home from the pubs at night, people urinated in the lifts or outside the high-rise building entrances.

In 1977, I decided to focus my PhD on the rise of the earliest cities in the Southern Levant, ca. 3000 to 2650 BCE. To do this, I planned a survey of 5th to 4th millennium BCE sites

THE BOOMER ARCHAEOLOGIST
• CHAPTER 16 •

along the Wadi Beersheva/Wadi Gaza (Nahal Besor) in Israel's Northern Negev Desert. Since the Six-Day War in 1967, Israeli archaeologists were mostly researching in the occupied Sinai Desert. As hardly anyone was working in Northern Negev, I selected Beersheva as my base. I soon met David Alon, the inspector of the region, who gave me permission (not a permit) to do the job. I could only afford a one-speed bike to carry out the survey. On one of the initial days, a guard at the Hatzerim Airbase fired a shot in my direction. I was scared "shitless," and so I quickly abandoned surveying in that area — for a while.

Back to the Holy Land, 1977

Lily and Uncle Tom on Phone Call

FREEZING LONDON

From the time you were 19 years old, your heart was set on doing your doctoral fieldwork in Greece. When that dream fell apart, how did you bounce back?

HOT AS HELL IN BORREGO SPRINGS

As I note here, my girlfriend, your Aunty Alina, played a major role in helping me overcome that bad phase. She has always been down-to-earth and clear-eyed. As plans for Israel rapidly came together, I was excited to return to my roots and move forward. So love and roots made me resilient.

THE BOOMER ARCHAEOLOGIST

CHAPTER 17

Copper Age Nirvana and Dad's Death, 1978

THE BOOMER ARCHAEOLOGIST
· CHAPTER 17 ·

My 1977 preliminary survey along the Wadi Beersheva was difficult, but a great success. In early 1978, I received a small research grant from my department in Sheffield and purchased an old Fiat mini-van for £350. I built a plywood bed in the back. Dr. Robin Dennell doubted if it would even make it out of Sheffield. By June, Alina and I named the vehicle "Alphonse," drove it to the Hovercraft at Folkestone, and were soon driving across Europe to Greece, where we would pick up the ferry to Haifa. We were 50 km from the Greek border in communist Yugoslavia (now Northern Macedonia) when Alphonse sprung

Copper Age Nirvana and Dad's Death, 1978

a leak in the engine block. My old Cuban neighbor in the Valley had told me that in such circumstances you should crack a fresh egg and drop it in the radiator. It would temporarily seal the leak. The hard part was for Alina. She had to ask our fellow campers, who spoke no English, for an egg. To our amazement, it worked, and we made it to a metal shop where a new part was fashioned by hand to repair the block.

THE BOOMER ARCHAEOLOGIST
• CHAPTER 17 •

Our plan on arriving in Israel was to find Alina a volunteer position at a kibbutz in the Negev and for me to join Professor Bill Dever's excavation at Be'er Resisim in central Negev to gain more field experience. The kibbutz office in Tel Aviv arranged for Alina to be at Urim in Northern Negev. After dropping her off at the kibbutz, I drove south to meet Dever's team. That night, Alina was assigned to the screwdriver factory, and she immediately fell in love with the kibbutz and its very successful brand of socialism.

I left Kibbutz Urim early in the morning and had a hard time locating Professor Dever's Early Bronze IV (ca. 2300–2000 BCE) site. Dever was excavating with Israeli archaeologist Rudolf (Rudy) Cohen. It was just before lunch when I arrived, so the archaeologists were still digging. When I found Dever at

Copper Age Nirvana and Dad's Death, 1978

the tent camp, he rushed up to me and said, "Tom, your Uncle Stephen called to say your father is dying and you need to return to Los Angeles ASAP." I immediately jumped into Alphonse and drove back to Kibbutz Urim to say goodbye to Alina.

10 months earlier, Dad had been diagnosed with cancer of the bile duct. Uncle Gene was in the operating room, and when it was discovered, he told the surgeon to sew Dad up, as further operating might kill him. The doctor gave my father 1 year to live. It was now month 11. A week after my arrival, Dad was still in good enough shape to invite me to lunch at our favorite deli. He leaned over the table and said, "Tom, I need to tell you something I never told your mother." I thought he was going to say that he had a mistress or something similar. Instead, he said that after serving with the 452nd Bomb Group in England, he was transferred to ground forces in Germany and was at

THE BOOMER ARCHAEOLOGIST
• CHAPTER 17 •

the liberation of the Dachau Concentration Camp. Dad said that he administered instant justice to the Nazis they found there. He lifted his hand and imitated a pistol, squeezing the trigger. Dad was not proud of this, however, he was satisfied he had done the right thing. Dad died on July 25, 1978, as we played his favorite Johnny Cash songs on the tape player. After losing Dad, I stayed on for a week to help my mother.

It is hard to imagine that some 40 years ago, without cellular phones and Google Earth, it was much harder to navigate and communicate around the world. This is why I didn't get to know how serious my father's health was, as we traveled

Copper Age Nirvana and Dad's Death, 1978

with Alphonse across Europe, until I arrived at Be'er Resisim. Alina and I were poor, so it was out of the question that she could accompany me home. However, Dad knew about Alina from my letters. When I arrived at the Los Angeles International Airport (LAX), I was amazed to see my father standing at the exit gate, waiting for me. We did not know that he would be dead in a month.

As soon as I arrived back in Israel, I went to Beersheva, took Alphonse, and drove to Urim to collect Alina. Thanks to Itzik Gilead, an archaeologist at Ben-Gurion University of the Negev, we stayed at the student dormitory with his colleague, the French prehistorian François Valla. They were doing a survey in the Yatir Forest. Alina and I used the dorms as our base. We traveled each day to a site I discovered, which David Alon actually found in 1950 but had forgotten about.

THE BOOMER ARCHAEOLOGIST
CHAPTER 17

David and I named the site "Shiqmim" (Sycamores) — after the tree near a Turkish well up the wadi. It took Alina and me 2 weeks to make a topographic map of the site using a Brunton compass and a builder's level. Shiqmim became the focus of my research up until 1993; I was obsessed with this amazing site, situated in a trough-shaped valley in the rolling loessial hills along the Wadi Beersheva. I thought of it as Chalcolithic "Nirvana," because it was otherworldly, emanating a kind of transcendent state because of the wealth of Copper Age artifacts and architectural remains on the surface — as if the inhabitants had recently left it. ✺

Copper Age Nirvana and Dad's Death, 1978

Lily and Uncle Tom on Email

RAINING CATS AND DOGS IN LONDON

I REALLY WISH I HAD MET YOUR DAD. YOU WERE ONLY 24 WHEN YOU LOST YOUR DAD; HOW DID THAT AFFECT YOU?

BRILLIANT SUNSHINE IN SAN DIEGO

I WAS GRATEFUL I WAS ABLE TO BE WITH MY FATHER FOR THE LAST MONTH OF HIS LIFE IN 1978. LOSING HIM MADE ME WANT TO RETURN TO ISRAEL QUICKLY, FOCUS ON WORK, AND EXCEL AS MUCH AS POSSIBLE. DEEP DOWN, I WANTED TO MAKE HIM PROUD OF ME. I WISH HE COULD HAVE JOINED ME ON MY EXPEDITIONS, HELPING ME BUILD AND MAINTAIN THINGS IN OUR VARIOUS CAMPS; HE WOULD HAVE LOVED IT.

THE BOOMER ARCHAEOLOGIST

THE BOOMER ARCHAEOLOGIST

THOMAS EVAN LEVY

• CHAPTER 18 •

The Man in the Desert Museum — Bedouins, 1979–1985

THE BOOMER ARCHAEOLOGIST
◦ CHAPTER 18 ◦

By 1979, Alina and I had fallen in love with Israel. Shortly after getting married (next chapter), Israel was our "last stop" — we became "Olim Hadashim" — new immigrants to an old land. My first job was with the Negev Museum in Beersheva, as their ethnographic curator of Bedouin culture. Alina got a job in the cytogenetics lab at Soroka Hospital. I was hired to establish the first museum of Bedouin culture in the Beersheva Municipality. It was to be called the "Man in the Desert Museum." Little did I know, I was becoming the "Man in the Desert," as there was no funding for the project for

The Man in the Desert Museum — Bedouins, 1979–1985

several years. Early on, the archaeology curator, Dr. Artu Segal and I were tasked with painting the mosque, as the municipality had no money to pay for exhibitions.

On March 26, 1979, the Israel-Egypt Peace Treaty was signed by Israeli Prime Minister Menachem Begin and Egyptian President Anwar Sadat — and by US President Jimmy Carter as a witness — at the White House. Consequently, Israel had to give back to Egypt the Sinai Peninsula it had captured in the Six-Day War of 1967. In terms of archaeology, with the redeployment of the Israel Defense Forces (IDF) from Sinai to the Negev Desert,

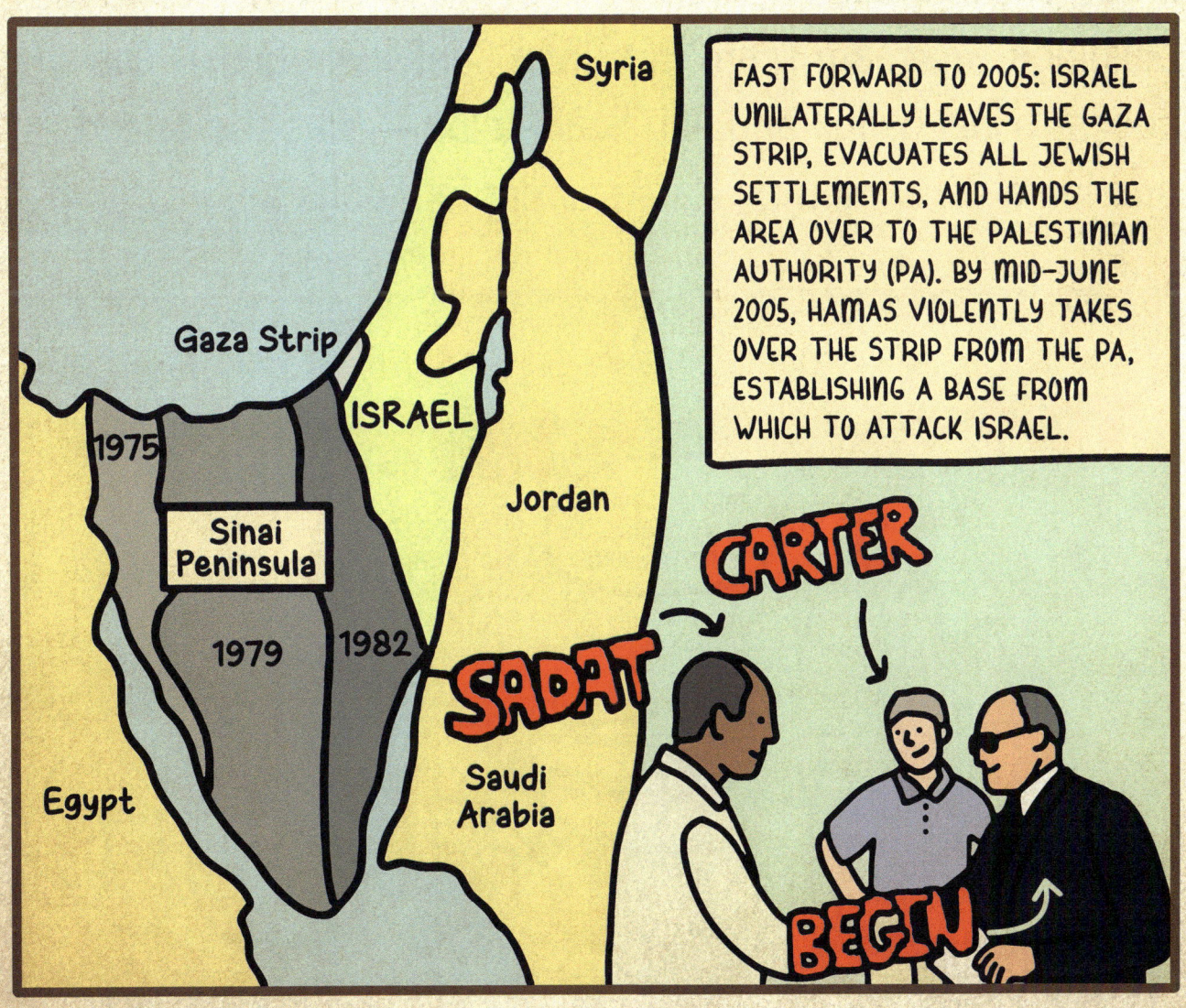

THE BOOMER ARCHAEOLOGIST
• CHAPTER 18 •

it meant that there would be massive archaeological surveys and excavations in the Negev areas where new military bases and exercise areas would be located. Personally, it meant that the Israeli archaeologists who were very active in the Sinai region became more interested in areas closer to home — like the Wadi Beersheva where I had surveyed for the past 2 years, especially in the Chalcolithic site of Shiqmim.

I spent the first year in Israel riding my bike every day from Beersheva to Tel Sheva, where the late excavator of Biblical Beersheva, Yohanan Aharoni, had his camp. The Man in the Desert Museum would be built in one of the abandoned buildings. Ghassam from the Tiâha Confederation — the Qderat tribal group and Abu Rqaiq tribe — was the guard, and his elderly mother, Watfa, spent her days at the camp.

The Man in the Desert Museum — Bedouins, 1979–1985

Watfa was the matriarch and beloved member of the tribe. Bedouin from near and far came to her campfire at the site for tea and advice. I learned a lot from her. I also had a short postdoc with the noted Israeli anthropologist Emanuel Marx — an expert on the Negev Bedouin.

While waiting for funding for the Man in the Desert Museum, I was free to do my archaeological research along the Wadi Beersheva. Professor Dever visited Alina and me in Beersheva, and was impressed by Shiqmim. Dever suggested that I apply to National Geographic, which I did, and in 1982 I received my first "large" grant! As Shiqmim was in the middle of an Israeli army firing zone, the army was extremely helpful. The commander of the local Tze'elim base, Colonel Moti Rosenberg, lent me army tents, giant ice boxes, water tanks, an army radio, and more.

THE BOOMER ARCHAEOLOGIST
• CHAPTER 18 •

I learned that the noted Israeli Bauhaus architect Arieh Sharon and his son, Eldar, had helped design exhibits in Israel. I went to their Tel Aviv office for advice. Among other pointers, they told me where in Tel Aviv to purchase "bouboat" (mannequins). The Beersheva Municipality agreed to the expensive purchase, and so I ordered 2 men, 2 women, and a child. As the bouboat were geared for Ashkenazi clientele at high-end shops, I had them painted in darker skin tones to match the Negev Bedouin. I found a Palestinian sign painter in Hebron and traveled there

The Man in the Desert Museum — Bedouins, 1979–1985

to have all the museum signs painted by hand in Arabic, Hebrew, and English. After 4 years, the museum opened to great fanfare, with the local Bedouin Sheikhs and the neighboring Bedouin community as chief guests.

After 5 years, Alina and I were fed up living in Beersheva, where my job had no future, and she was starting an MSc degree at the prestigious Weizmann Institute of Science in Rehovot. In July 1985, Seymour (Sy) Gitin, the director of the W.F. Albright Institute of Archaeological Research in Jerusalem, where I had just finished a National Endowment for the Humanities postdoc, offered me the job of Assistant Director. This was "manna from heaven," and it meant that Alina, our Boxer pup Sandy, and I would be living in Arab East Jerusalem for 2 years. We were excited! ✡

THE BOOMER ARCHAEOLOGIST

CHAPTER 19

Marriage and Tribe, 1978–1979

THE BOOMER ARCHAEOLOGIST
• CHAPTER 19 •

In the 1970s, Alina was one of the few Asian students at the University of Sheffield. In those days, it was extremely rare for an Indian woman to have a non-Indian boyfriend, let alone a boy who was invited to stay overnight in his girlfriend's house. Alina's mom, Noemia, and dad, Alirio, were incredibly open-minded. The fact that I was Jewish, and the family devout Catholics, made no difference to them. On numerous occasions when Alina invited me home to London, I volunteered to work in their "Newsagents" shop in Tooting Bec, selling cigarettes, candy, and newspapers. I was always amazed when Noemia

Marriage & Tribe, 1978–1979

placed a £10 note in my hand at the end of the day. I felt ecstatic every time I earned some cash so that Alina and I could prepare for our road trip to Israel.

At the beginning of 1977, Ben-Gurion University (BGU) of the Negev was very kind in letting me stay in the "Moanoat Gimel" student dorm, which became the base for my survey of the Wadi Beersheva-Wadi Gaza. After I returned from Los Angeles, I picked Alina up from Kibbutz Urim, and BGU

THE BOOMER ARCHAEOLOGIST
• CHAPTER 19 •

let her move in with me. Itzik Gilead from BGU and French archaeologist Francois Valla were doing a survey in the Yatir forest. Alina endeared herself to the group as she volunteered to cook — and she is an awesome cook. On Friday afternoons, Francois would treat Alina and me to a steak lunch in Beersheva. Saturday mornings we would wake up and find an envelope filled with shekel notes slipped under our door from a mysterious patron (Francois).

Life seemed great to me. By the end of August, Alina received a letter at the dorm offering her a job at a bookshop in London, which could lead to a career at the British Broadcasting Corporation (BBC). One afternoon she said, "Yeah, everything is great except our future together. You need to commit to me if we are going to stay together." That was when Alina proposed marriage to me, and I accepted, with one condition.

Marriage & Tribe, 1978–1979

I knew my family would not travel to the United Kingdom for our wedding, so we got married in Los Angeles. Alina completed the conversion process with Rabbi Steve Jacobs from my old synagogue, Temple Judea; Steve also solemnized our marriage. We married on the hottest day in California's recorded history — June 10, 1979, in Steve and Evie's backyard. My mother organized the entire wedding. Alina's mom, Aunt Judy, sister Yvonne, brother Allan, sister-in-law Lyne, and friends they knew from Africa were our wedding guests. My dad had passed away the previous year, and Alina's father had to stay home running the shop on Balham High Road. Alina officially became part of our tribe.

We returned to Israel after the wedding. Alina and I were happy in the Moanoat. One evening Itzik knocked on the door, and I discovered a sheepish look on his face. He said that we would have to move out soon. I said, "OK, tomorrow." Itzik said,

THE BOOMER ARCHAEOLOGIST
• CHAPTER 19 •

"You have to leave in an hour." BGU had been trying to take Shiqmim away from David and me. When they realized that was impossible, they gave Alina and me the boot. Fortunately, our friend Uri said that we could spend the night at his place. The next day we found an apartment in the run-down neighborhood of Shikun Dalet near Mercaz Gilat.

We could not afford a refrigerator. Every time we needed something fresh, we would go to the local "makolet" (shop) to buy yogurt, cheese, and such that would last for the day. Life was tough, but we were young and in love...

Marriage & Tribe, 1978–1979

In August 1979, Alina and I returned to Israel from Los Angeles as new immigrants (Olim Hadashim). The Ministry of Interior gave us some problems after realizing Alina's conversion by a Reform rabbi. However, I went to the Hebrew Union College in Jerusalem, met with Rabbi Uri Herscher, and he put us in touch with a lawyer in Tel Aviv. Thereafter, the State of Israel quickly recognized Alina as a Jew — problem solved! By September, David Alon and I realized that to hold on to Shiqmim, we had to conduct an "emergency excavation." We did so during the Jewish holidays, but without coordination with the Army. Late one afternoon, as we finished excavating, the entire landscape got enveloped by tanks, jeeps, armored personnel carriers, and soldiers. A commander found us hunkered down in the excavation and told us, "Get the hell out of here."

THE BOOMER ARCHAEOLOGIST

THOMAS EVAN LEVY

• CHAPTER 20 •

The People's Army — IDF, 1984–1992

THE BOOMER ARCHAEOLOGIST
• CHAPTER 20 •

By 1982, thanks to Bill Dever's visit to us in Beersheva, and his advice, I applied and received my first National Geographic grant! Alina helped me organize the finances and logistics for the project — a system that I have used until recently. I borrowed equipment from the Department of Antiquities, Hebrew Union College and the École Biblique in Jerusalem. Thanks to Étienne Nodet, the equipment included a mining train used by French archaeologist Père Roland de Vaux in 1946 at Tell el-Far'ah (North). We camped around 2 km

The People's Army — IDF, 1984-1992

upstream from Shiqmim, using an old Turkish trading post for our field lab. To entertain the team, I convinced our friends Eric Drucker and Leon Milo from the Beersheva Sinfonietta to give a concert to the team. This was a romantic setting, but not practical for fieldwork.

The following year, I thought I got smart and moved the camp downstream, directly adjacent to Shiqmim. When Ibrahim al-Assam, a young Bedouin volunteer from Tel Sheva looked at the camp, he said to Alina, "Why did Tom set up the camp next to the Wadi? In addition to flash floods, there will be tons of mosquitos." Ibrahim was right. The next year, I put the camp up on the hill overlooking Shiqmim, where we had cool afternoon breezes, no mosquitoes, and no danger of flash floods.

THE BOOMER ARCHAEOLOGIST
▫ CHAPTER 20 ▫

By the end of the 1984 expedition, I had enough data to produce the first multidisciplinary anthropological archaeology monograph of a post-Neolithic site in the Levant. I modeled it on Kent Flannery's 1976 study, "The Early Mesoamerican Village." My book laid the foundation for our understanding of the Beersheva Valley Chalcolithic as one of the earliest chiefdoms in the Southern Levant.

In November 1984, after living in Israel as a new immigrant for 4 years, at the age of 29, I was drafted into the Israel Defense Forces (IDF). At the time, 18-year-old recruits

The People's Army — IDF, 1984–1992

had a service tenure in the IDF of 3 years for men and 2 years for women. "Oldies" like myself did "Shlav Bet" — a shortened army service for older soldiers. I underwent the same 6-week basic training as all soldiers, followed by another 6-week specialist course. Thereafter, we served in the reserve army like everyone in Israel. My commanders were 19 and 20 years old. Our graduation consisted of a late afternoon 20-km march that ended in the evening at the Biblical site of Shomron (Samaria) in the West Bank. The site was the capital of the Israelite Kingdom.

When we arrived at Shomron, exhausted from the march, there were burning torches surrounding the Roman-period theater that was decorated with Israeli flags. None of our families could attend the ceremony due to security concerns.

THE BOOMER ARCHAEOLOGIST
• CHAPTER 20 •

When I was called up to receive my copy of the Hebrew Bible and M-16 rifle, it was announced that I was one of the 2 soldiers who were awarded "Excellent Soldier" from our unit. I was honored to receive this recognition, and moved by the Hebrew dedication that a young female officer had written in our Bibles by hand. It read: "In honor of completion of your basic training, class of February 9, 1985." "And they will beat their swords into plowshares and their spears into pruning hooks. Nation will not lift up the sword against nation, and never again will they learn war." (Isaiah 2:4). Our unit was then moved down to the Negev Desert for artillery training.

Having a PhD meant nothing in the IDF. I was assigned to the artillery corps as a simple soldier. After completing the basic course in artillery at Shivta — an ancient Nabataean town in the Negev Desert — I was placed in a reserve combat "miluim" unit whose base was in the Golan Heights. Our weapon

The People's Army — IDF, 1984–1992

was the American M109 "Doher" (Galloper) self-propelled 155 mm Howitzer. People from all walks of life were in my unit — a young professor of Yiddish from the Hebrew University, entrepreneurs, and the unemployed. My best friend was Johnny Harmetz — an American graduate from Yale who later became a kibbutz farmer. After 3 months of training in the IDF, I had lived in a tent for more than 5 months that year.

Living in Israel in the '80s and early '90s meant leaving your job and family behind to serve in the IDF every year for 1 to 2 months in miluim. From December 1987 until Alina, the boys,

THE BOOMER ARCHAEOLOGIST
CHAPTER 20

and I left for the USA, the first Palestinian Intifada (uprising) was raging. Before that, we patrolled the Syrian and Jordanian borders. During the Intifada, our unit served on the West Bank for a month or so each year, dealing with riots, apprehending terrorists, and more. Later in the year, we were again called up for a week of artillery exercises in the Golan Heights and Negev Desert. Having been active in the "Peace Now" movement in Beersheva, serving in the West Bank had many ethical challenges for me and everyone in our unit, no matter what their political orientation. We discussed the "situation" often and openly. ✡

The People's Army — IDF, 1984–1992

Lily and Uncle Tom on Phone Video Call

SUNNY LONDON

UNCLE TOM, DO YOU HAVE ANY REGRETS ABOUT HAVING SERVED IN THE IDF?

SUNNY SAN DIEGO

NOT AT ALL, LILY. SERVING IN THE ISRAEL DEFENSE FORCES WAS A VERY POSITIVE EXPERIENCE FOR ME; ONE THAT I'M PROUD OF. THE IDF IS THE TRUE EQUALIZER IN ISRAELI SOCIETY WHERE YOU MEET PEOPLE FROM ALL WALKS OF LIFE. WITH A YOUNG FAMILY, I FELT COMPELLED TO PLAY MY SMALL PART IN THE DEFENSE OF THE ONLY JEWISH STATE. MY RESERVE DUTY DID NOT TAKE PLACE DURING A WAR OR IN THE THEN OCCUPATION ZONE IN SOUTHERN LEBANON. SO MY ARMY EXPERIENCES, WHILE OFTEN INTENSE, DID NOT LEAD TO PTSD.

THE BOOMER ARCHAEOLOGIST

THOMAS EVAN LEVY

• CHAPTER 21 •

East Jerusalem and the W.F. Albright Institute, 1985–1987

THE BOOMER ARCHAEOLOGIST
• CHAPTER 21 •

It was a time of hyperinflation in Israel, when very low salaries and lack of academic opportunities in Beersheva compelled us to leave town in 1985. The offer to work in Jerusalem as Sy Gitin's Assistant Director at the W.F. Albright Institute of Archaeological Research was too good to be true. Hiring me would give Sy time to work on his publications while I ran the institute. I learnt a lot from Sy about administering an American research center. All the leading American archaeologists, and their students who visted Jerusalem, hung out at the Albright. One day, Geoffrey M. Shipton, one of the last pre-WWII staff members of the University of Chicago's Megiddo excavation team, came for tea.

My appointment included a salary higher than anything I received in Beersheva, and free accommodation at the

East Jerusalem and the W.F. Albright Institute, 1985–1987

Albright Institute in the basement apartment below the director's house. As it was being redecorated, Sy allowed Alina and me to have a say on some of the design. By July 1985, we had moved in with our Boxer Sandy. We became especially close to the Palestinian staff: Said Freij, the majordomo; Omar Jabrin, the long-term cook; Munira Said, the institute secretary; Fais, the gardener; and others. We visited their homes and celebrated holidays together.

We loved living in East Jerusalem and felt very comfortable being Jewish there. Our national health clinic (Kupat Holim) was located in the Jewish Quarter, so it was a treat to walk from the Albright down Salah ed-Din Street to the

THE BOOMER ARCHAEOLOGIST
• CHAPTER 21 •

Damascus Gate and through the ancient streets of the Old City. Omar had been the cook since the 1930s when Nelson Glueck served as director and the Institute was called the American School of Oriental Studies. Being a twice-displaced Palestinian from the 1948 and 1967 wars, Omar was a fount of local history, had wry humor, and a very unique perspective on life. One day, there was rioting around the Albright and the Israeli Border Patrol tried to bring order. They chased a guy into the Albright's back garden. Omar said, "If this was under Jordanian control, their army would have mowed these Palestinians down with machine guns."

East Jerusalem and the W.F. Albright Institute, 1985–1987

With the Albright job, I didn't do any archaeological fieldwork in 1985–86. However, during this period I was called up to miluim and had to return to the Albright (my home) in my uniform, carrying a rifle. Doing this in East Jerusalem, the Arab side of the city, was challenging. When the Palestinian workers and friends saw me in the Albright garden in uniform, I was incredibly moved when they insisted that I join them for hugs.

My appointment did not include the lovely meals prepared by Omar and his sons for the Albright residents. My favorite was the Palestinian dish "Maqluba" — upside-down chicken

THE BOOMER ARCHAEOLOGIST
◦ CHAPTER 21 ◦

with pine nuts. Omar couldn't understand this arrangement and made a point every evening after dinner of piling up plates of food — one for Alina, one for me, and a third one with scraps for Sandy. One of Omar's sons would deliver these welcome treats to our door. Running the Albright day to day was not that difficult. There were remodeling jobs to oversee, salaries to be paid, grounds to be inspected, seminars to organize, and more. However, I had time to focus on my research. I applied to the National Endowment for the Humanities and received a major grant for the phase II exploration of the earliest layers at Shiqmim. At nights I would return to the office to use the HP computer system to typeset my first book — the monograph "Shiqmim I" that summarized my 1979 and 1982–84 fieldwork — published in 1987, shortly after I left Albright. ✦

East Jerusalem and the W.F. Albright Institute, 1985–1987

Lily and Uncle Tom on Computer Video Call

VILLA ALINA, GOA

HOW DID SERVING AS THE ASSISTANT DIRECTOR OF THE ALBRIGHT INSTITUTE AFFECT YOUR CAREER PATH?

HOME, SAN DIEGO

AS A YOUNG MAN, I LEARNED A LOT ABOUT WORKING WITH DONORS AND ORGANIZING A SMALL RESEARCH INSTITUTE FROM SY GITIN, THE ALBRIGHT DIRECTOR WHO HIRED ME. FOR ME, WORKING IN THE FOOTSTEPS OF GREAT AMERICAN SCHOLARS WHO HAD DIRECTED THE INSTITUTE IN THE EARLY YEARS, SUCH AS W.F. ALBRIGHT AND NELSON GLUECK, WAS A SOURCE OF PRIDE. IT INSTILLED IN ME A COMMITMENT TO HELPING PROMOTE EXCELLENCE IN AMERICAN ARCHAEOLOGICAL RESEARCH IN THE HOLY LAND; A GOAL THAT CONTINUED IN MY CAREER AS A PROFESSOR.

THE BOOMER ARCHAEOLOGIST

CHAPTER 22

West Jerusalem and the Nelson Glueck School for Biblical Archaeology, 1987–1992

THE BOOMER ARCHAEOLOGIST
• CHAPTER 22 •

Philanthropists are amazing people. Every philanthropist has their own reasons for giving back to society. The Jewish community has the tradition of "Tikkun Olam" — "repair the world" — and Jews tend to give something to others regardless of their income level. I have been blessed to know some extraordinary and wealthy philanthropists — people from diverse backgrounds.

West Jerusalem and the Nelson Glueck School for Biblical Archaeology, 1987–1992

When my contract at the Albright Institute ended, Richard J. "Dick" Scheuer, Chairman of the Board of Governors of the Hebrew Union College - Jewish Institute of Religion (HUC-JIR), and a supporter of the Albright, reached out to Professor Avraham Biran, Director of the Nelson Glueck School of Biblical Archaeology (NGSBA) at HUC-JIR in Jerusalem. Dick said to Biran, "If the Albright can have an Assistant Director, don't you think NGSBA can?" I soon received a call from Professor Biran and I moved seamlessly into my new job as Biran's Assistant Director.

Dick's mission was to develop liberal Judaism in a pluralistic, Jewish State of Israel; this was grounded in Dick's passion for Biblical history and archaeology, and his vision to expand the HUC-JIR Jerusalem campus. I think Dick appreciated my passion for fieldwork and commitment to publication.

Professor Biran was one of the founders of the modern State of Israel. When the British ruled Palestine in the 1930s, they appointed Jews to help administer Jewish areas and Arabs for Arab regions. Biran was made district officer of the valley of Beth Shean. One day he was driving his car with a British policeman seated next to him, and in the back seat were Chaim Sturman, head of settlements, his friend Aharon Erkin, and veterinary officer David Mossenson. Terrorists planted a mine on the road, and Biran drove over it. The resultant blast killed all 3 in the back seat; Biran and the police officer walked away.

THE BOOMER ARCHAEOLOGIST
• CHAPTER 22 •

After the 1948 Arab-Israeli war and the ensuing independence of Israel, Biran was appointed the deputy military governor of Jerusalem. By the mid-1950s, he became Israel's consul general in Los Angeles and, in the early 1960s, the director of the Department of Antiquities (now the Israel Antiquities Authority). When he retired at the age of 67, he became the director of the NGSBA — a post he held until he was 94!

West Jerusalem and the Nelson Glueck School for Biblical Archaeology, 1987–1992

The spectacular HUC-JIR Jerusalem campus came to fruition with the partnership of Dick Scheuer and the renowned architect, Moshe Safdie, who long ago had been a student of the great Jewish-American architect, Louis Kahn. Thanks to the Skirball Foundation, an entire building was built for archaeology and Biblical studies. My office was across the hall from Professor Biran and his secretary, Hanni Hirsch.

THE BOOMER ARCHAEOLOGIST
• CHAPTER 22 •

Professor Biran knew that I was a prehistorian and wanted me to "hit the ground running" in Biblical archaeology. As Biblical archaeology was thought to have begun in the Chalcolithic period, when I joined the HUC-JIR in 1987, Biran suggested that I work with David Alon and expand excavations in the Chalcolithic temple at Gilat. Biran funded the excavation, and we found fantastic ritual objects, including scores of violin-shaped figurines made of stone and "torpedo" vessels used to store valuable olive oil.

West Jerusalem and the Nelson Glueck School for Biblical Archaeology, 1987–1992

After the success of the 1987 field season at Gilat, I recommended to Professor Biran that we needed new tents, generators, and more field equipment — all very expensive. I suggested to Biran that it would be a great idea if I sent a request letter to Dick Scheuer. "Try it," said Biran.

6 weeks later, the president of HUC-JIR, Alfred Gottschalk, came to Jerusalem and stayed on campus in Nelson Glueck's palatial apartment. I received a message that the president wanted to see me immediately. I ran up to the apartment, looking forward to meeting him. After being ushered in, I was summarily chewed out. Lesson learned.

THE BOOMER ARCHAEOLOGIST
• CHAPTER 22 •

West Jerusalem and the Nelson Glueck School for Biblical Archaeology, 1987–1992

One day in May 1988, Professor Biran yelled out from his desk for me to see him. When I entered his office, Biran waved a magazine in one hand to show me the cover of a cowboy banker holding his llama. Agitated, Biran said, "Oy Vey! What am I supposed to do with this guy? A friend from the Israel Bonds said that this guy — C. Paul Johnson — loves Israel, is not Jewish, is not a practicing Christian, and doesn't even like the Bible. However, he doesn't want to buy bonds; he wants to support an archaeology dig here. What do I do with him?"

I quickly looked at the C. Paul Johnson file and saw he loved Southwestern Archaeology in the USA, so I said, "This guy will love the Chalcolithic period," to which Biran said, "Fine, take him on a week-long tour of all the active digs in Israel and let him choose what he wants to support." ✡

THOMAS EVAN LEVY

• CHAPTER 23 •

Beautiful Boys — Ben and Gil, 1988

THE BOOMER ARCHAEOLOGIST
CHAPTER 23

You get married, buy an apartment, and have kids. That is what you expect; that is what is supposed to happen. In 1983, Alina got pregnant, and we were on top of the world for several weeks until we discovered it was an ectopic pregnancy, which had to be terminated. Depression set in for us, and the long road to years of fertility treatment began. By 1988, we decided to adopt children. At the time, many Israelis were adopting children from Central America. We decided that for us, as Jews, why go far away when there were children in Israel who needed a home and parents?

Beautiful Boys — Ben & Gil, 1988

Alina and I were excited to adopt a baby from Israel. Our social worker, Yona, met us and excitedly said, "We found the perfect children for you! They are biological brothers, aged 4 and 5, who have been in the children's home for 2 years and have never been abused, but the biological parents had drugs, alcohol, and other problems. For 2 years, the biological family had not visited the boys. The boys have suffered emotionally from this rejection. They are extremely intelligent and beautiful, and desperately need an 'Ema' (mother) and 'Abba' (father)."

THE BOOMER ARCHAEOLOGIST
• CHAPTER 23 •

As potential adoptive parents, over several months, Alina and I had taken the mandatory battery of psychological tests and courses on rearing children. Yona said, "You are the ideal parents. If you want an infant, it is very difficult. However, if you are willing to adopt these small boys, who cannot be separated as they are brothers, you can do it in less than a month." Alina and I looked at each other and said "OK." Yona would arrange for us to meet the boys at one of our friends' homes in Tel Aviv. If the 4 of us liked each other, the adoptions would proceed. I had just been called up for miluim in the Negev. Yona said, "I will call the Chief of Staff of the army and make sure you will be free to meet the boys." Sure enough, a week later, on August 7, 1988, Alina and I drove to Tel Aviv and met the boys. We took them for pizza and fell in love with them instantly. The next day we picked the boys up to take them to our home in Jerusalem

Beautiful Boys — Ben & Gil, 1988

Adoption legislation mandated that we change the boys' names and get them entered in our identity cards. As per the legal process, we had to give time for the biological family to challenge the adoption, and so we could not travel outside of Israel for 2 years. No one ever came forward, and after the waiting period was over, the 4 of us went to the Jerusalem court. The judge asked Ben and Gil, "Do you boys want Alina and Tom to be your Ema and Abba?" The boys said, "YES!" Case closed. A new chapter opened — we became their proud, legal family.

THE BOOMER ARCHAEOLOGIST
◦ CHAPTER 23 ◦

At the time of the adoption, we were living at the Hebrew Union College. The staff loved the boys. Rahamim Goren, the majordomo, whom I had first met at Tel Gezer in 1971, and his wife, Etti, were especially warm to the boys. Moshe Safdie's expansive courtyard was great for biking.

Beautiful Boys — Ben & Gil, 1988

A month after the boys arrived, we took them to join us on the Shiqmim expedition. This meant that they would live with us in a tent camp in the Northern Negev Desert for a month and a half. Yona thought we were crazy, but the boys loved the experience. Throughout their childhood, Ben and Gil joined us on many expeditions in Israel and Jordan. ✡

THE BOOMER ARCHAEOLOGIST

THOMAS EVAN LEVY

CHAPTER 24

Warring Chiefdoms from the Banks of the Wadi Beersheva, 1987–1993

Warring Chiefdoms from the Banks of the Wadi Beersheva, 1987–1993

By 1987, I had secured major funding from the National Geographic Society and the National Endowment for the Humanities for a 3-year project to explore the rise of the earliest chiefdom in the Southern Levant, based on our excavations at Shiqmim. A chiefdom is a regional polity with a 2-tier settlement hierarchy (a large village center with smaller satellite sites) that was fueled by chiefly control over food surpluses and craft specialization. Chiefdoms led directly to the rise of the first cities and early civilizations.

My early surveys along the Wadi Beersheva and Wadi Gaza, and excavations at Shiqmim, put my work at the center of scholarly debates as to whether my team and I had indeed found the earliest chiefdom in our region. By late September 1986, I assembled an interdisciplinary team and volunteers from around the world to explore the earliest strata at Shiqmim and the rise of social complexity. We camped on a chalk hilltop opposite the Shiqmim site. I appointed Ibrahim Al-A'asam as camp manager. Ibrahim's tribe is part of the Qderat tribal group, of the Tiâha Confederation. They adopted me as part of the Al-A'asam tribe. I visit Ibrahim and the family every time I'm in Israel.

THE BOOMER ARCHAEOLOGIST
• CHAPTER 24 •

While we were in the field, a gravel extraction company was digging in the wadi. On our arrival they had cut into Shiqmim. Although the site was damaged, the tractor cut showed that there were underground rooms at the site! We began excavating north of this tractor trench and found a copper workshop just below the surface. Soon a pit emerged. It went down over 3 m. This tunnel led to over 10 underground rooms filled with storage silos, pottery vessels, and prestige objects. It was very dangerous excavating underground. My best excavator was Yoav Arbel, who eventually went on to do a PhD with me at UCSD.

Warring Chiefdoms from the Banks of the Wadi Beersheva, 1987–1993

One afternoon, Alina and I were driving back to Shiqmim in our jeep. Suddenly, we saw an Israeli Air Force jet in the distance plunging down, and then we heard a giant explosion. Alina started to cry, and then we saw two parachutes descending to earth. When the plane hit the ground, there was a huge fireball — a backdrop to the many gazelles that sprung up against the turbulence in the desert landscape.

THE BOOMER ARCHAEOLOGIST
• CHAPTER 24 •

I put the jeep in gear, and we raced to where the parachutes came down. We found the pilot and navigator collecting their aerial photos that were scattered around their ejected seats. "Can we help you?" I asked. "No thanks, just some water, please. The rescue chopper will be here in 5 minutes. You guys should leave now." As soon as the jet crashed into the desert, the Bedouins — scavenging for parts — reached the crash site, and the Israeli Air Force rapidly took charge of the area to prevent those parts from being smuggled across the border into Egypt. Thus began a wonderful relationship with the rescue chopper pilot, Major Raz, whom our students affectionately called "Rasbo," after the popular movie star character "Rambo." Every day for a week, Raz would land his chopper on the hilltop next to our tent camp. He would have coffee with us and then fly off to continue investigating the crash. One day

Warring Chiefdoms from the Banks of the Wadi Beersheva, 1987–1993

I asked him if he would fly us around so that I could take the first aerial photos of Shiqmim. "No problem," said Razbo, and soon Alina and I were airborne over the wadi.

In mid-October, there was a rainstorm in the southern Judean mountains. It rained in the night, and our excavation was covered with pools of water. I called off work that day (very rare for me) and told the volunteers not to venture near the wadi, as there might be a flash flood. Ibrahim and I walked down to inspect the site and saw three students stuck in the middle of the wadi as the water rose around them rapidly. I told Ibrahim to run to the camp and fetch rope and staff to help with the rescue. Thanks to Ibrahim, he reached the Spanish students stuck in the middle of the wadi in time for them to pull themselves to safety with the rope we held. Ibrahim was almost swept away! I was tempted to expel the students from the project, but I did not.

THE BOOMER ARCHAEOLOGIST
- CHAPTER 24 -

Warring Chiefdoms from the Banks of the Wadi Beersheva, 1987–1993

By 1993, I teamed up with an amazing geophysicist, Alan Witten, who had worked for years at the Oak Ridge National Laboratory in Tennessee. Alan got increasingly interested in archaeology. At Shiqmim, we applied his method of Geophysical Diffraction Tomography (GDT) for imaging under the hills. Alan's method was featured in the movie "Jurassic Park." We discovered that the hills of Shiqmim were permeated with underground room complexes extending for half a kilometer. Finally, we had evidence of the 2 main economic drivers of chiefdoms: central control of surplus food or staple goods stored underground and a prestige economy based on the control of craft specialization in metallurgy, ivory, ceramics, and beautiful basalt vessels.

My longest collaborator on the Shiqmim project, besides David Alon, was Yorke Rowan, who began as a volunteer in 1984, and we continue to work together along with my first successful PhD student — Margie Burton, who did her PhD on the ceramics from Shiqmim. Since 2015, Margie has been a science project manager on 2 of my major grants: the UC Office of the President Catalyst Grant and the Koret Foundation Grant.

THOMAS EVAN LEVY

· CHAPTER 25 ·

The Archaeology of Cult: 1987, 1990–1992

THE BOOMER ARCHAEOLOGIST
CHAPTER 25

In the spring of 1987, Professor Biran tasked me with giving the Chicago banker — C. Paul Johnson, his wife Anne, and daughter Julie — a tour of the major archaeological excavations going on in Israel at that time. Paul would decide which project to support. After a week of visiting sites, including Gilat, where David Alon joined us, we went to Masada in the Judean Desert — where, according to the Roman-Jewish historian Flavius Josephus, almost 1,000 Jews committed mass suicide instead of surrendering to the Roman troops. Hiking down the Masada mountain as the sun was setting, Paul said, "Tom, pull over; we need to talk. The chairman of the board in the sky has decided that you and I are going to work together." I was elated. Thus

The Archaeology of Cult: 1987, 1990–1992

began Paul's generous support for my work, mostly in Israel, and for a few years in Jordan from 1987 to 2001. We remained good friends until Paul's untimely death in 2015. In my book "The Archaeology of Society in the Holy Land," based on a conference that I organized shortly after arriving at UC San Diego, which Paul helped support, I dedicated the book to "C. Paul Johnson — a great American."

In 1990, David Alon and I started a large-scale project at Gilat in the Northern Negev, which Paul supported. David was an amazing man, and I was especially close to him. He and his wife, Leah, were pioneers of Kibbutz Mishmar HaNegev, founded on the eve of Passover, 1946. They had 4 children; the oldest, Gil, was killed on the last day of the 1967 Six-Day War, in Sinai. David and Leah were devasted by the loss. As a kibbutz member, David helped edit — along with Amos Oz, Abba Kovner, and others — the book "The Seventh Day: Soldiers' Talk about the Six-Day War" (1970, Penguin). David began his archaeology as an amateur collector, exploring the Negev on his days off. Later he earned a BA and MA in archaeology and became the regional inspector of Northern Negev archaeology. After working together for 14 years, David said, "Tom, the longer we work together, the more Western I become and the more Middle Eastern you get." David was very close to the local Bedouin, especially the et-Turi family, who regarded him as a father figure.

THE BOOMER ARCHAEOLOGIST
• CHAPTER 25 •

DAVID AND TOM AT GILAT

Our work at Gilat brought together a fantastic group of scholars. The leading expert on Chalcolithic pottery, Catherine Commenge; on petrography (sourcing where pottery was made), Yuval Goren; on human remains, Patricia Smith; on marine and riverine shells, Daniella Bar-Yosef; on archaeozoology, Caroline Grigson; and on flint and ground stone tools, Yorke Rowan. Thousands of artifacts at Gilat indicated ritual acts. Based on organic residue analysis, my first PhD student, Margie Burton,

The Archaeology of Cult: 1987, 1990-1992

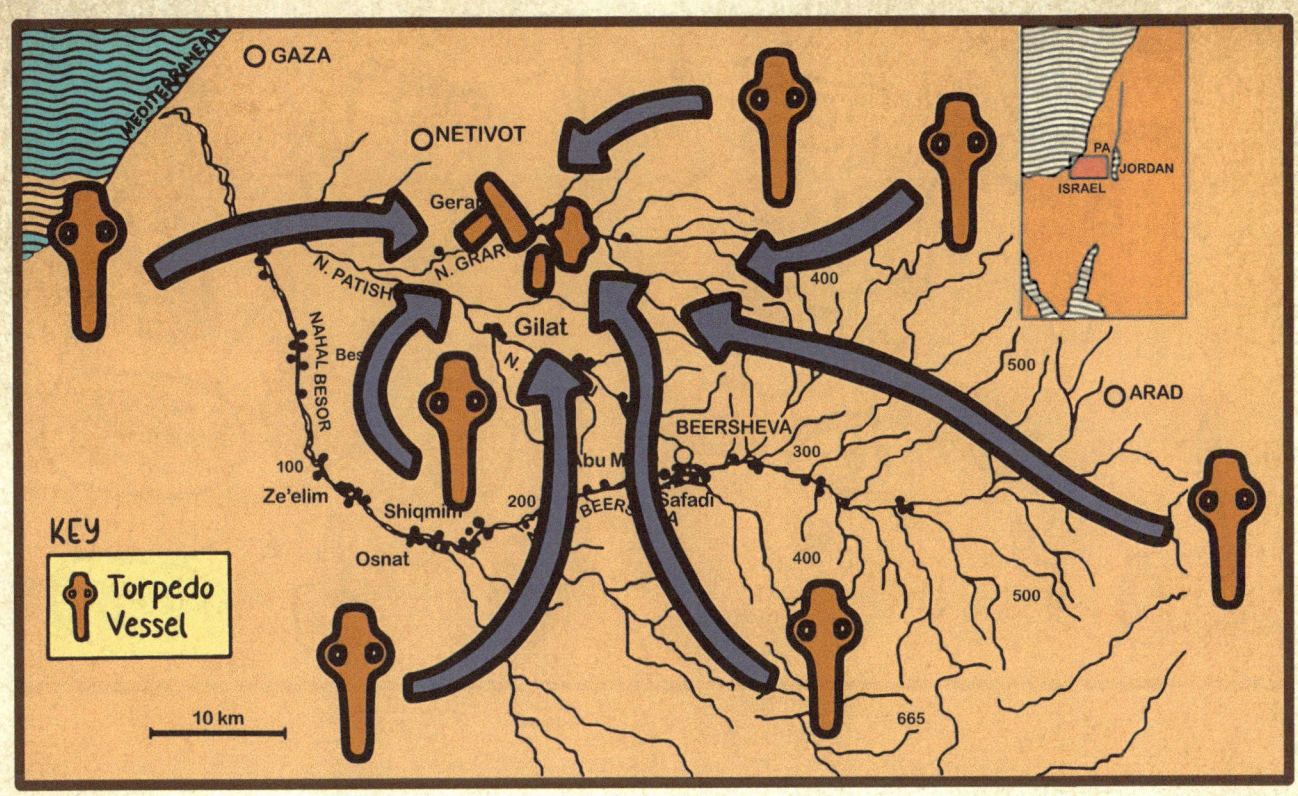

showed that unique "torpedo" storage jars found only at Gilat contained olive oil. Goren's petrographic study of these pots showed that they were made in at least 7 different areas of the Southern Levant. This meant that they were brought to Gilat from many regions as offerings of olive oil to the temple.

To date, the earliest temples in the Holy Land belong to the Chalcolithic period, and only 3 have been found: Teleilat Ghassul to the northeast of the Dead Sea, Ein Gedi on the west coast of the Dead Sea, and Gilat. They all had a special "holy of holies" room and a courtyard that foreshadowed later temples in the ancient Near East, including Solomon's Temple. I was extremely fortunate to have been invited to excavate Gilat by David. The holy of holies contained the "Gilat Woman" and "Gilat Ram" — emblematic of the importance of milk and other secondary

THE BOOMER ARCHAEOLOGIST
• CHAPTER 25 •

animal products at the time. Offerings and raw materials, such as the violin-shaped figurines, were brought to Gilat from other geographic regions. Excavations at Gilat produced the largest number of these beautiful stone figurines for any site in the Southern Levant. Many of these objects are on permanent display at The Israel Museum in Jerusalem.

I published a final monograph on the Gilat excavations called "Archaeology, Anthropology and Cult: The Sanctuary at Gilat, Israel." I don't think many people ever read it — quite typical of academic publications! Personally, I think it is a tour de force for understanding the role of ritual and religion in the rise of social complexity and the maintenance of a vibrant society. Already during the main occupation (Stratum IIC), when the Gilat Woman and Gilat Ram were worshipped in the holy of holies, people wanted to be buried near them. We found

The Archaeology of Cult: 1987, 1990-1992

8 human burials there. In the following occupation period, more than 20 burials were found there, showing the continued growth of the ritual pilgrimage center.

For the Gilat book, I invited prominent cultural anthropologists to provide models of how traditional societies in New Guinea (Donald "Don" Tuzin), the Bedouin in Sinai (Emanuel Marx), and followers of the Jewish North African rabbi, Baba Sali (Yoram Bilu), created ritual centers that provided the social glue for their communities. In analyzing the Chalcolithic sanctuary at Gilat, I found the anthropologist Victor Turner's ideas helpful; for instance, "Religion is the key to culture, and ritual is the key to religion for understanding Gilat." This idea still works in the 21st century, except where societies have given up on religion, like in Western countries. During our 1990 season, I went home to Jerusalem one weekend and stopped at HUC-JIR.

THE BOOMER ARCHAEOLOGIST
• CHAPTER 25 •

I needed a book from Professor Biran's office. I happened to see a letter on his desk from the Dean, Michael Klein. It asked, "Shall we award Tom Levy tenure at HUC?" I was shocked to read in Professor Biran's very clear handwriting — "No." I went home and told Alina, who responded, "You need to find a job outside of Israel." ✡

The Archaeology of Cult: 1987, 1990–1992

Lily and Uncle Tom on Email

LILY'S LONDON KITCHEN TABLE

DID YOU RESENT PROFESSOR BIRAN FOR REFUSING TO SUPPORT YOU GETTING TENURE AT THE JERUSALEM CAMPUS?

TOM'S HOME OFFICE

I WAS SHOCKED WHEN I DISCOVERED PROFESSOR BIRAN DIDN'T WANT TO GIVE ME TENURE. HOWEVER, I KNEW EVEN IN HIS EARLY '80s, BIRAN DID NOT WANT TO RELINQUISH HIS DIRECTORSHIP OF THE NELSON GLUECK SCHOOL OF BIBLICAL ARCHAEOLOGY TO A YOUNG SCHOLAR. I ALWAYS RESPECTED HIM AS A FOUNDER OF THE STATE OF ISRAEL AND AS A SENIOR ISRAELI ARCHAEOLOGIST. BIRAN ALWAYS GAVE ME THE FREEDOM TO CARRY OUT MY RESEARCH AND IT WAS FUN TO BE AROUND HIM; HE ALSO TAUGHT ME A LOT ABOUT PUBLIC LECTURING AND FUNDRAISING. I NEVER RESENTED BIRAN AND REMAINED FRIENDLY WITH HIM UNTIL HE PASSED AWAY IN 2007. THANKS TO PROFESSOR BIRAN, I ENDED UP AT A MAJOR AMERICAN RESEARCH UNIVERSITY WITH OPPORTUNITIES I NEVER WOULD HAVE HAD IN ISRAEL.

THE BOOMER ARCHAEOLOGIST

THE BOOMER ARCHAEOLOGIST

CHAPTER 26

Terror in Baka, 1990

THE BOOMER ARCHAEOLOGIST
• CHAPTER 26 •

Central to Judaism, Christianity, and Islam, living in Jerusalem is like residing in the center of the universe. In 1989, our 2 years of free accommodation at HUC-JIR on King David Street ended.

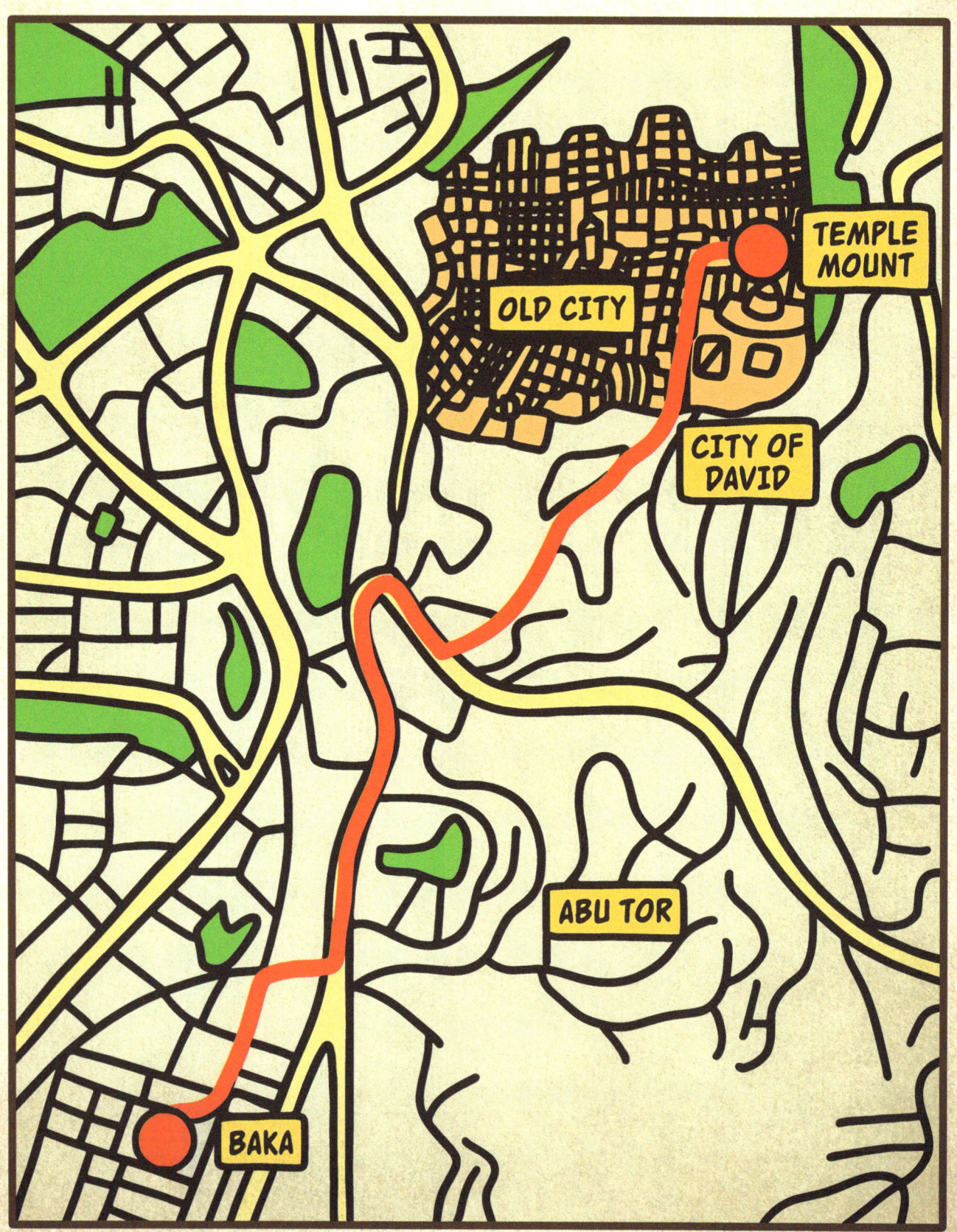

Terror in Baka, 1990

We moved into the Baka neighborhood, a 40-minute walk from the Old City and Temple Mount. Baka was established late in the 19th century for wealthy Muslim, Christian, and Armenian families from the Old City who built homes there after the completion of the Jerusalem Railway Station in the 1920s. After the 1948 Arab-Israeli war, it fell on the west-Israeli side of divided Jerusalem. We found a tiny but attractive 65 m² rooftop flat in a 2-storey stone Bauhaus building, designed by a Jewish architect, overlooking a vacant lot.

In October 1990, my friend and colleague, Dutch Egyptologist Edwin van den Brink, invited me to a conference in Cairo. It could have been my first visit to Egypt! A day before my

THE BOOMER ARCHAEOLOGIST
• CHAPTER 26 •

planned departure, Alina had a dream the night before I was supposed to leave, and she said, emphatically, that I should not go to Egypt. This was totally out of the ordinary, as Alina had never suggested me to cancel a trip. However, I agreed and dropped out of the conference.

October 20, 1990: The previous evening, we had a lovely dinner prepared by Alina. We decided to let the boys sleep in and hang out with us. Around 7 a.m. on a Sunday morning, we heard terrible screams from outside our window.

Terror in Baka, 1990

A 19-year-old Palestinian, who had worked in our neighborhood for some time and knew many of the Jewish neighbors, decided to carry out revenge for the death of 21 Palestinians on the Temple Mount (Haram al-Sharif in Arabic) some weeks before. He started by stabbing to death an 18-year-old unarmed girl soldier, Iris Azulai, outside her house. He tried to attack a 13-year-old boy but was chased off by a dog. Walking toward our building, the terrorist chased our 43-year-old neighbor, Eli Alturatz. Eli owned a plant nursery and was a member of Peace Now. Eli was slaughtered not far from the entrance to our building. When Charlie Shlush — our neighbor and member of the "Yamam" anti-terrorist squad — heard the

THE BOOMER ARCHAEOLOGIST
◦ CHAPTER 26 ◦

commotion, he rushed downstairs, cornered the guy, and shot one round in the air with his official gun. When the terrorist didn't relent, Charlie shot him between the legs, taking care not to kill him. Charlie thought he had "neutralized" the guy, who dropped his commando knife. Charlie approached to arrest him, but the terrorist pulled out a hidden knife, stabbing 26-year-old Charlie to death.

Around 7:30 a.m., we went downstairs with the boys to walk them to school. Yael, Charlie's 9-month pregnant wife, came down to the yard where around 8 local Sephardi women had cornered the terrorist and were waiting for the police. Yael arrived and said, "Don't worry, Charlie is here, all will be OK." Then Yael looked at the shoes protruding from under the white sheet. "Oh my God! That's Charlie!" Yael gave birth to Shirli a week later. We had to walk past Eli's body, covered

Terror in Baka, 1990

by a sheet. Ben and Gil saw everything. When they got to school, there already was a team of psychologists on hand to help the neighborhood children. Gil drew a remarkable picture of what he had seen that morning. ✿

THE BOOMER ARCHAEOLOGIST

THOMAS EVAN LEVY

• CHAPTER 27 •

From Ethnoarchaeology in Cameroon to the Gulf War

THE BOOMER ARCHAEOLOGIST
- CHAPTER 27 -

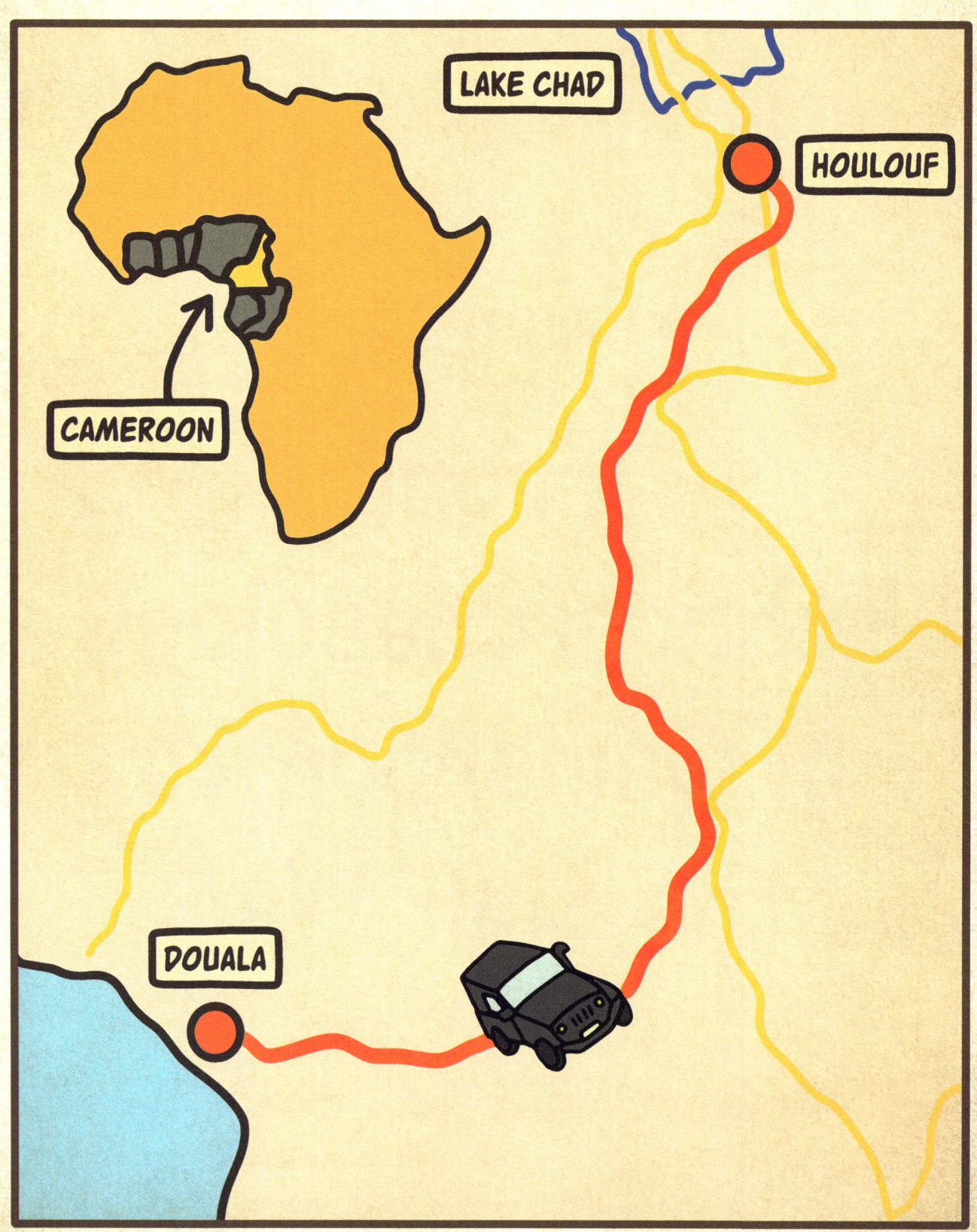

From Ethnoarchaeology in Cameroon to the Gulf War

I first met Augustin Holl in 1982 at a conference hosted by The Prehistoric Society in London. I had recently completed my PhD and presented a paper on the Wadi Beersheva, concerning the Chalcolithic chiefdom I discovered. After my speech, Augustin introduced himself, saying he had similarly identified an ancient Chadic chiefdom at Houlouf in Northern Cameroon. While I was trained in Sheffield and Augustin at the Sorbonne in Paris, our approaches (socio-economic) to anthropological archaeology were remarkably similar. We became fast friends, and I invited him to participate in my excavations in Israel. To my surprise, he showed up in Beersheva some months later to join the Shiqmim project. Augustin was an awesome excavator. When I published the Shiqmim I volume, I invited Augustin to lead a chapter on household archaeology. In 1988, Augustin invited me to join his project in Houlouf with the idea that I would lead the ethnoarchaeological study of contemporary Shuwa Arab pastoralists, who were undergoing the transition from a nomadic to a sedentary society. This remains an important issue in studying the evolution of social complexity. Our second season was in late December, 1990.

THE BOOMER ARCHAEOLOGIST
• CHAPTER 27 •

I have always believed that anthropologists are the curators of culture — past and present. Unfortunately, most cultural anthropologists in the USA today have lost interest in the traditional locus of anthropology — small-scale societies. In the USA, they have mostly retreated from those areas of the world where traditional culture is found, often afraid to venture far from an American university campus — let alone travel abroad. Today, archaeologists, with their interest in material culture, are the anthropologists who are most interested in small-scale societies. As Augustin worked for many years in Northern Cameroon, excavating, he saw the potential of an ethnoarchaeology study of the local nomadic Shuwa Arabs. I felt honored and excited to kick-start that study, which resulted in a number of joint publications. It took us 3 days of travel time by train and a 4WD Toyota Land Cruiser to reach the study area. We first paid our respects to the paramount chief — the Sultan of the settled Kotoko tribe in the town of Logone-Birni.

We started work by systematically excavating an abandoned Shuwa Arab hut — just like good old-fashioned archaeologists. Our crew was made up of 8 Shuwa Arab young men who crammed into the back of our 4x4 each day. On the second day of "digging," our workers said, "Why dig? We can ask our grandparents if you can come to our abandoned village and study without digging." Listening carefully, I had just shoveled a log off the collapsed roundhouse when a giant Nile monitor lizard, around 4 feet long, jumped out. I now thought it was a great idea to leave the digging behind and focus on investigating the many seasonally abandoned Shuwa Arab villages.

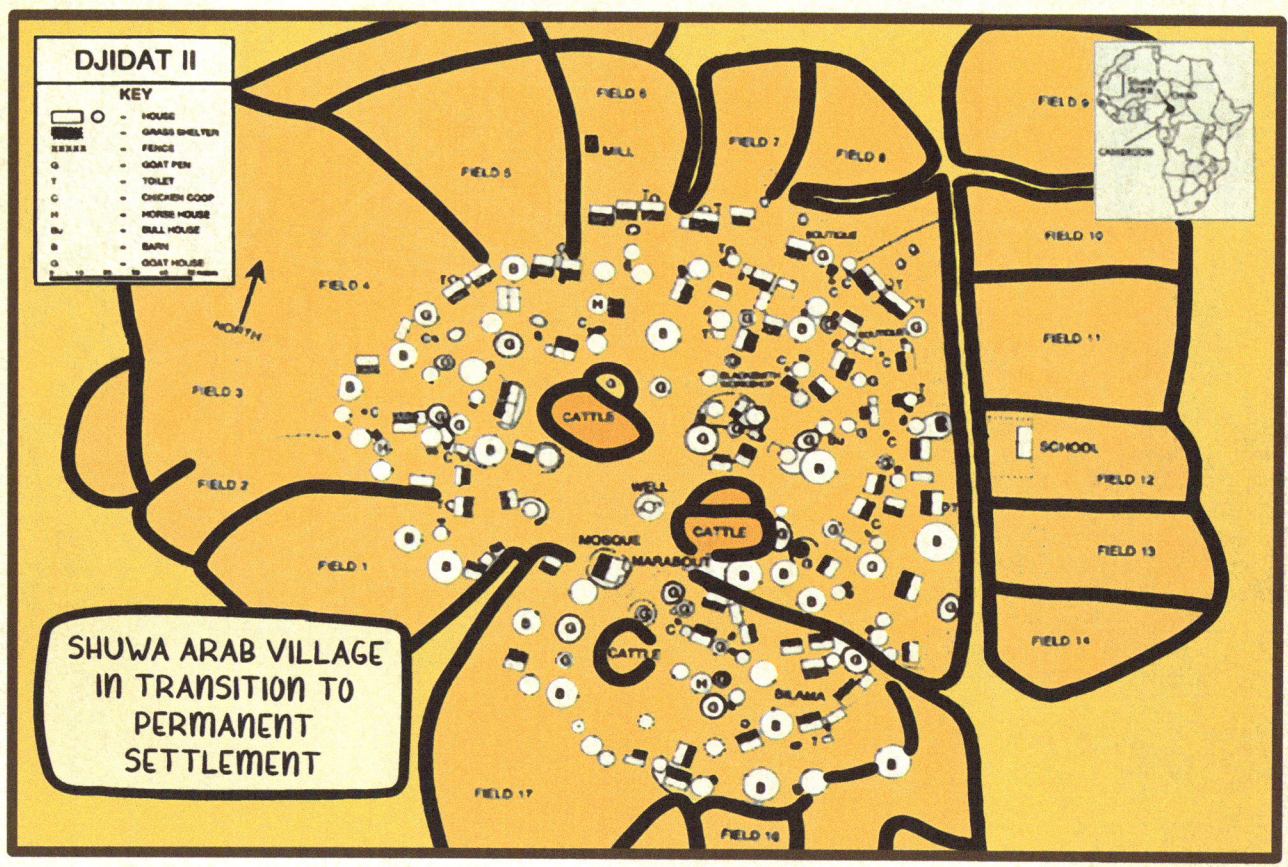

SHUWA ARAB VILLAGE IN TRANSITION TO PERMANENT SETTLEMENT

Like the transition from Upper Paleolithic hunters and foragers to sedentary Neolithic farmers, we documented the rise of a new Shuwa Arab regional settlement that competed with the traditional permanent Kotoko villages and towns. We mapped the shift from circular huts made of brush to mudbrick rectilinear houses made by specialists using our compasses and tape measures.

From Ethnoarchaeology in Cameroon to the Gulf War

Alina and the boys stayed in London while I was in Cameroon. In the last days of the expedition, the First Gulf War broke out after Iraq's Saddam Hussein invaded neighboring Kuwait. From January 17 to February 23, 1991, Iraqi forces fired 42 Scud missiles on Israel. The fear was that Saddam would fire chemical weapons on Israel. In deference to the USA, Israel did not respond, as the Americans were concerned that Israeli action would upset Arab members of the coalition against Saddam. On our arrival at Ben Gurion Airport in Tel Aviv, there was a blackout, and we were handed gas masks. We spent the last week of the war hunkering down in our safe room at home in Jerusalem, donning gas masks every time the sirens went off.

THOMAS EVAN LEVY

• CHAPTER 28 •

The Golden Medina, 1992

THE BOOMER ARCHAEOLOGIST
• CHAPTER 28 •

Early in 1992, Gary Rollefson — then a professor at San Diego State University — had lunch with Guillermo Algaze from UCSD, who said there was a job opening at UCSD for an anthropological "Biblical archaeologist." Fortunately, Gary kindly posted me an express letter with this news, and I immediately applied. This was pre-internet and pre-fax days. I was an undergrad in the 1970s when Gary was a grad student

The Golden Medina, 1992

at the U of A, specializing in Levantine prehistory. In April 1992, we were excavating at Gilat. Alina was working in Jerusalem and at home with the boys. Professor David Jordan from the UCSD Department of Anthropology called, and he wanted to speak with me immediately. Alina called the local "makolet" at Gilat and arranged for David to call me there the next day. When we spoke, David invited me to San Diego for a job talk and interviews. I was elated! UCSD put me up in a nice La Jolla hotel. The first night, I thought of our life in Jerusalem. The second night, looking out at the Pacific Ocean, I thought, "This could be good." The day before leaving for Israel, I was offered the job. Back in Israel, I bumped into Ruth Amiran, a pioneer and leading Israeli archaeologist. I had worked with Ruth at her famous excavations at Tel Arad, and she and her husband, David Amiran, were very kind to us. When Ruth saw me at The Israel Museum, she was very upset with my decision to take the job in California.

Lacking what Israelis call "Vitamin P" ("Protektzia," favoritism in English), I had no chance of getting a tenure-track university job in Israel, as I hadn't studied under any Israeli professors — nor did my teachers. The only reason we left Israel was so that I could get a decent job. In July, we arrived at LAX — where my mom, Aunt Doshie, and Uncle Gene were waiting for us. Our biggest worry was for Sandy to arrive safely from the long flight. We almost lost her in Zurich when they took her crate off the plane and we heard over the loudspeaker, "Will Sandy Levy please come see the manager immediately!"

We rented a U-Haul truck, filled it with free furniture from my family in Los Angeles, and the 5 of us piled in to drive down the Pacific Coast Highway to the stunning La Jolla. After 3 months, we bought our first home in University City near UCSD. We soon discovered that when UCSD was established, Jews were not allowed to live in La Jolla, so planners built the University City neighborhood, expecting Jewish faculty to reside there. Thanks to Jonas Salk, who established the Salk Institute in La Jolla, Jews were welcome anywhere in San Diego by the time we got there. The "Bio-Tech" revolution was peaking, and Alina immediately got a job close to home, at Canji — America!

The Golden Medina, 1992

My appointment came through Judaic Studies and Anthropology. At the time, UCSD had excellence in both these fields. Anthropology was founded by Melford Spiro, a cultural and psychological anthropologist. I actually took Mel's book, "Children of the Kibbutz," with me to Israel in 1971 for an independent study I carried out there. Mel was still at UCSD when I arrived, and for years we only spoke Hebrew together. UCSD was in the top 10 anthropology departments in the USA when I arrived, and Judaic Studies had one of the most respected Biblical Studies programs as well.

THE BOOMER ARCHAEOLOGIST
• CHAPTER 28 •

Thanks to the largess of the local San Diego Jewish community, especially Miriam and Jerry Katzin, the Judaic Studies program had millions of dollars in endowments. For a period, Judaic Studies had more (6!) endowed chairs than any department at UCSD. Richard Elliott Friedman worked closely with Jerry to build the program. When a chair was created for the noted Hebrew Bible scholar David Noel Freedman, Noel insisted that a specialist in Northwest Semitic languages and a Biblical archaeologist be hired. UCSD agreed and that is how my position was created. We had awesome weekly faculty-graduate student Judaic Studies seminars. Together we became one of the top Hebrew Bible/Archaeology programs in the USA. My colleagues were incredibly supportive, and 1 year after my arrival, they provided funds (along with C. Paul Johnson!) to host the first international conference on socio-economic perspectives on the archaeology of the Levant. Transcending history, the +30

The Golden Medina, 1992

leading researchers resulted in a landmark book still widely used, which covers the earliest prehistory to World War I.

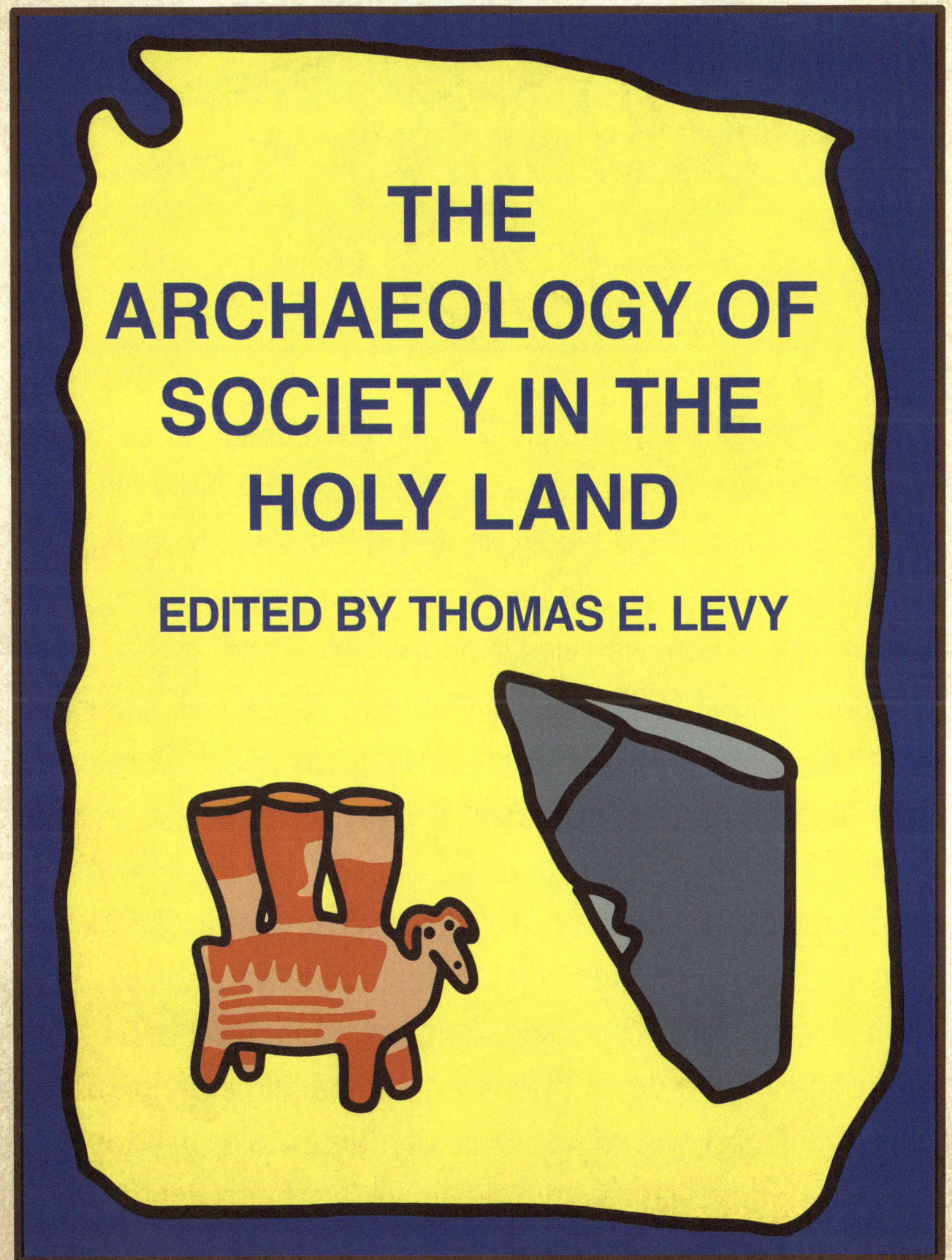

Source: https://www.academia.edu/34345588/ARCHAEOLOGY_OF_SOCIETY_IN_THE_HOLY_LAND_Edited_by_T_E_Levy

THE BOOMER ARCHAEOLOGIST
• CHAPTER 28 •

In the '90s, UCSD promoted itself as a meritocracy, emblematic of the American dream. When I was hired, the Anthropology Department asked if I really wanted the Assistant Professor job. This was because I had a very strong publication record for my age. My answer was emphatically, "Yes!" 2 years after arriving at UCSD, I was evaluated for tenure (Associate Professor). To my surprise, my colleagues in Anthropology nominated me for "Full Professor," and my case was successful. At the time, only 2 UCSD faculty "skipped" the Associate Professor rank — Michael Freedman from Mathematics (who won the prestigious Fields Medal in 1986), and me. On promotion, my Anthropology colleagues wanted me to be the next chair of the department. I could hardly say no. In retrospect, this and my drive to continue fieldwork took too much time away from my family. As chair (September 1997 to August 2000), I wanted to jump-start a PhD program in archaeology. I worked hard to recruit my old friend, Augustin Holl, then a young professor at the University of Paris (Nanterre). Augustin was well-published and a leading expert in African archaeology. Thanks to Augustin, our PhD program began immediately upon his arrival, and the program does well today. To date, I have supervised 15 successful PhD students.

THE BOOMER ARCHAEOLOGIST

THOMAS EVAN LEVY

• CHAPTER 29 •

Earliest Egyptian Colonization in Canaan, Nahal Tillah, 1994–1996

THE BOOMER ARCHAEOLOGIST
• CHAPTER 29 •

The Southern Levant has always been the land bridge between Africa and Asia. By 1994, I had spent 17 years working on the Chalcolithic period and the rise and maintenance of chiefdoms. Many archaeologists spent their entire career focused on one period; now I wanted to understand what happened after these highly successful societies collapsed. Did the emergence of Egyptian civilization in the Early Bronze Age (EBA), around 3600-3000 BCE, have something to do with it? It was time to research the Early Bronze Age.

Earliest Egyptian Colonization in Canaan, Nahal Tillah, 1994–1996

The ideal place to study the transition to the EBA was at Kibbutz Lahav, located 32 km to the northeast of Shiqmim. Joe Seger, who co-directed the Gezer excavation when I was there, and his team found evidence of the Chalcolithic/EBA transition near the Kibbutz gate, as did David Alon when he made an emergency dig in the area. I faxed David from San Diego, suggesting we start a regional project and call it "Nahal Tillah" after a small wadi that flows into the Biblical Nahal Grar to the west of the kibbutz. Like Shiqmim, we opened an extensive area to understand the plan of the settlement. From 1994–1996, we discovered extensive evidence for an EB IB (ca. 3300–3000 BCE) and Egyptian presence at the site.

Our excavations at Lahav revealed amazing data from Dynasty One, when Egypt was unified by King Narmer and other early pharaohs. This included an incised pot sherd with Narmer's

THE BOOMER ARCHAEOLOGIST
• CHAPTER 29 •

name! It was made of Nile Valley clay and consisted of an incised Serekh — a rectangular enclosure representing the niched or gated façade of a palace and courtyard. Inside is the "n'r" (catfish) symbol of Narmer's name. The same Serekh sign is seen on the famous Narmer Palette, now on display at The Egyptian Museum, Cairo. This means there was direct trade between the earliest Egyptian dynasty and our site at Lahav. In 1996, our last excavation season, Egyptologist Edwin van den Brink and I organized an international conference in

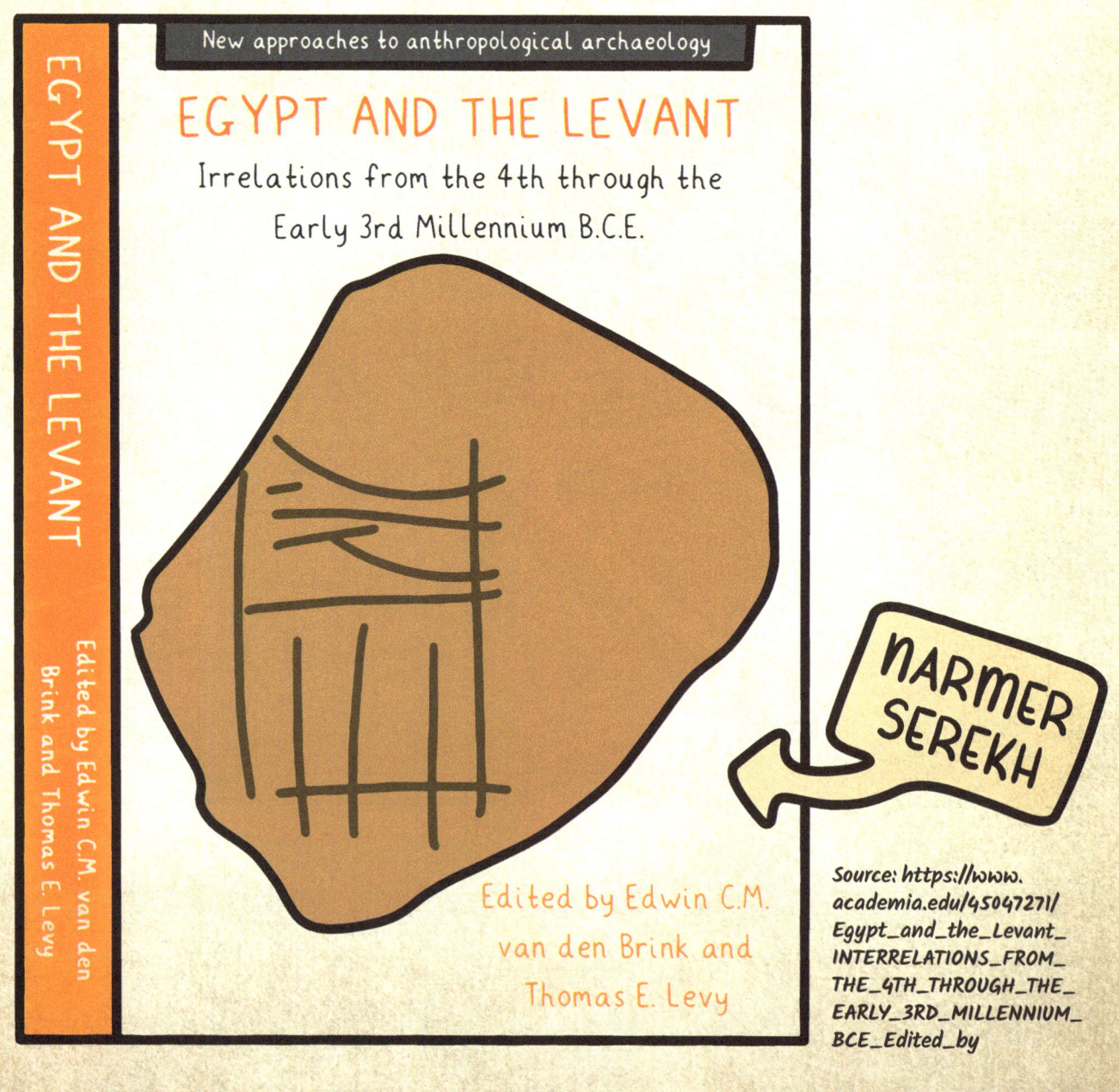

Source: https://www.academia.edu/45047271/Egypt_and_the_Levant_INTERRELATIONS_FROM_THE_4TH_THROUGH_THE_EARLY_3RD_MILLENNIUM_BCE_Edited_by

Earliest Egyptian Colonization in Canaan, Nahal Tillah, 1994–1996

Jerusalem with over 30 experts, to understand the nature of Dynasty One Egyptian-Levantine interaction. The book came out in 2002 and has a lot of our project data in it.

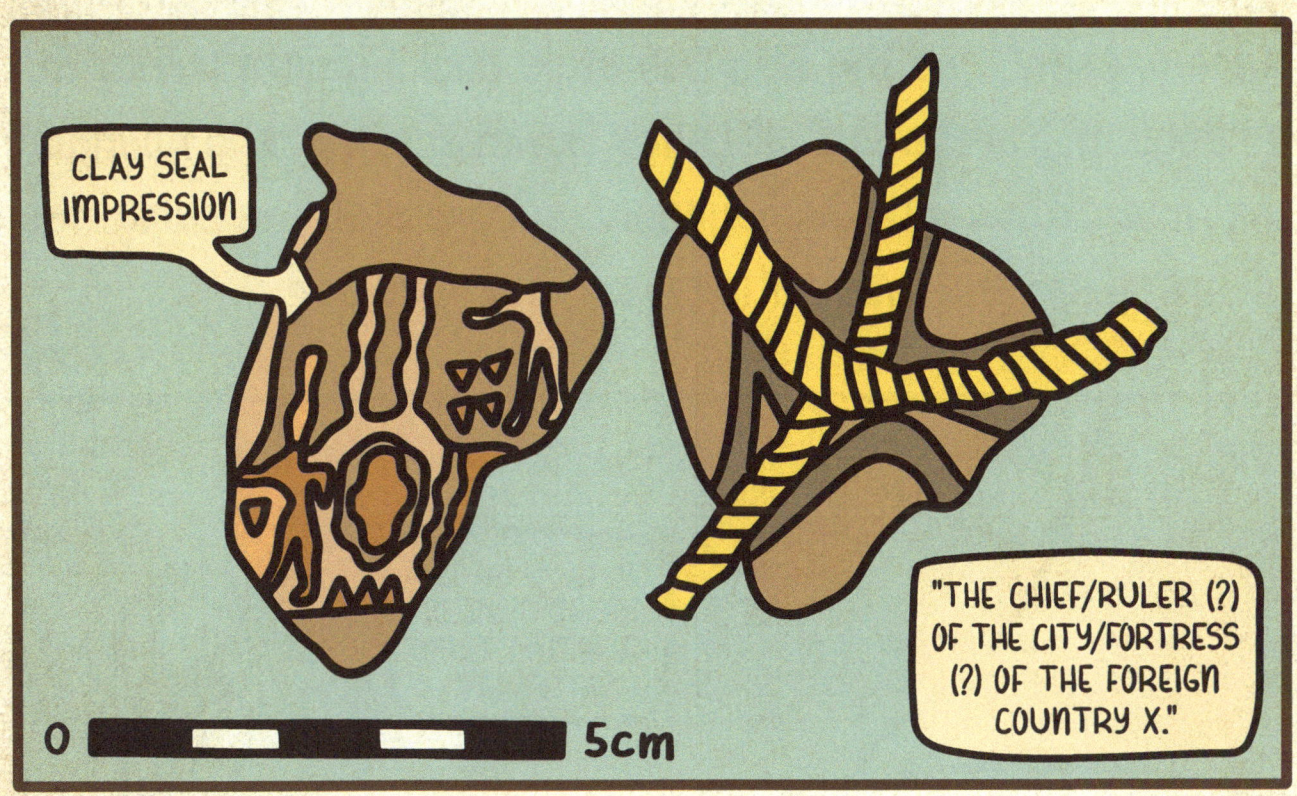

Food is equal to ethnicity and tribe. At Nahal Tillah, I worked closely with Edwin, who read one of our seal impressions made on local clay. It probably sealed a jar, as seen from string impressions on the back. The seal shows that Lahav had direct exchange with King Narmer's court and highlights that our site was a fortress or city around 3300–3000 BCE. We identified an Egyptian "neighborhood" at Lahav based on thousands of bread mold fragments and ovens, typical of Dynasty One Egypt. We also found a monumental tomb like those from Dynasty One at Helwan. Our sons, Ben and Gil, helped excavate it. What were the Dynasty One Egyptians doing at Lahav?

THE BOOMER ARCHAEOLOGIST
• CHAPTER 29 •

To understand the Egyptian presence, scholars have suggested many ideas: peer (equal) polity interaction, warfare and conquest, colonization, trade diasporas, and more. We don't have a definitive answer, but the tomb suggests Egyptian elites were present, and the Egyptian style cooking data points to a range of "foreigners" at Lahav. Howevers, there is no doubt that interaction with the Egyptians accelerated the early rise of urbanism and internationalism in our region.

Earliest Egyptian Colonization in Canaan, Nahal Tillah, 1994–1996

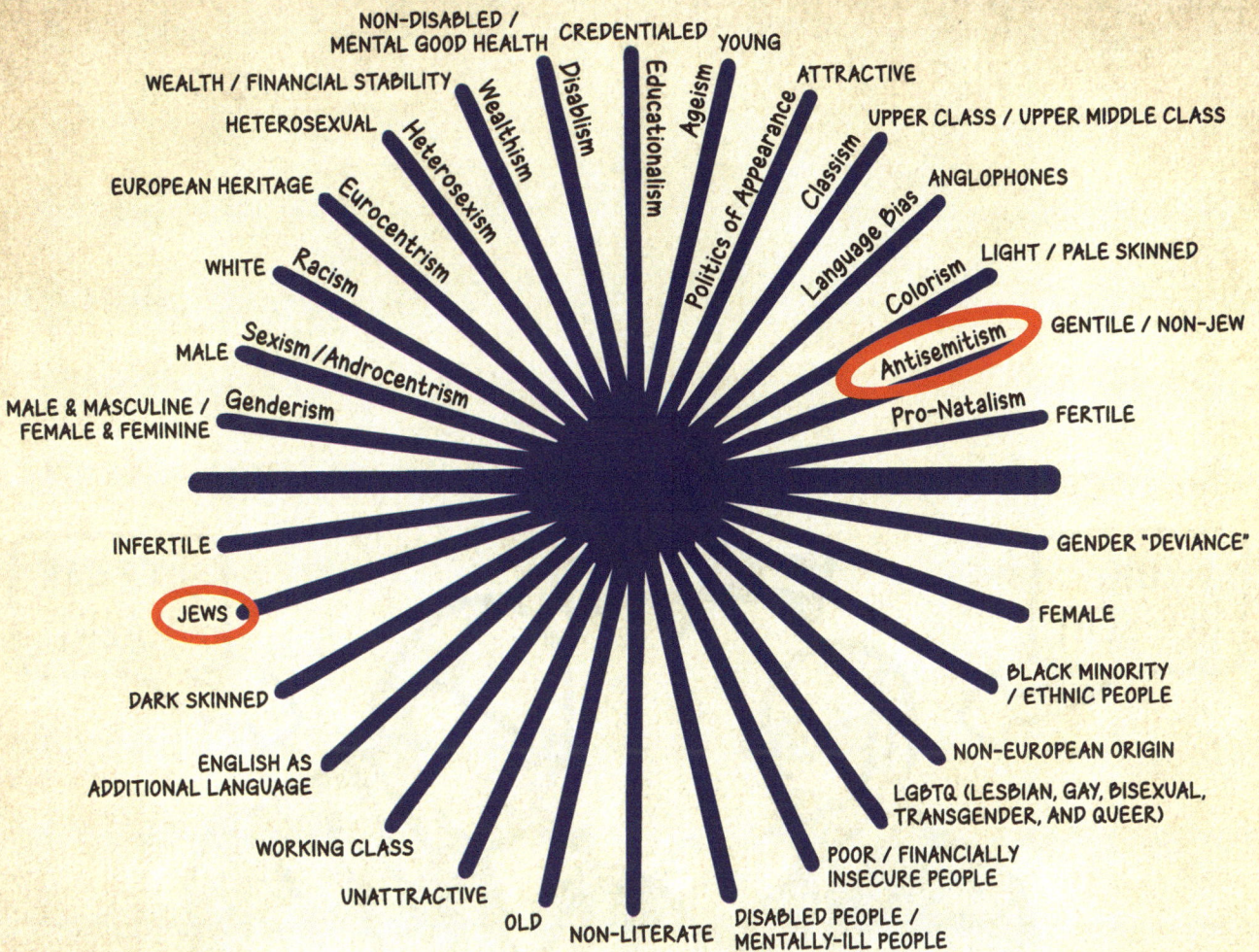

Meanwhile, back in San Diego... The 1990s were a great time to be a Jewish scholar in America. All over the USA, generous Jewish donors endowed chairs in Jewish Studies, contributed to university buildings, and much more. My life experience dovetailed with Kimberlé Crenshaw's recent 1989 model of Intersectionality, where American Jews were part of the oppressed due to antisemitism. Our families always reached out to other communities. Although Jews embraced the "American Dream," and prospered in the US by taking advantage of it, their history and constant threat of antisemitism put Jews on the side of the dominated classes. This is how I viewed the place of Jews in American society after having lived for 16 years abroad.

THE BOOMER ARCHAEOLOGIST

CHAPTER 30

Crossing Jordan, 1997

Jordan-Israel Peace Treaty, October 26, 1994

THE BOOMER ARCHAEOLOGIST
• CHAPTER 30 •

At the end of the 1996 excavation, less than 2 years after the historic Jordan-Israel peace treaty, Pierre Bikai, Director of the American Center of Oriental Research (ACOR) in Amman, visited Israel and Kibbutz Lahav, where I was excavating. Pierre and noted Jordanian architect Ammar Khammash came to investigate joint Jordanian-Israeli tourism around the Dead Sea. After giving Pierre a tour of our site, he said, "Tom, you should work in Jordan." When I explained I had never been to an Arab country, he said, "You will love it. If you rent a jeep, I'll drive and show you the country so you can pick a place to excavate."

Crossing Jordan, 1997
Jordan-Israel Peace Treaty, October 26, 1994

I fell in love with Jordan and chose the Wadi Faynan region in southern Jordan, as that was the source of the copper we found at Shiqmim. When I explained to Ghazi Bisheh, Director General of the Jordanian Department of Antiquities, that I had worked for 20 years in Israel, he said "Mafi Mushkila — No Problem." In early 1997, National Geographic asked me to advise them on a Chalcolithic article they were writing. I was flown to Washington, D.C., and gave lectures for 2 days. When I explained how Chalcolithic people mined copper in Faynan and transported it to the Wadi Beersheva by donkeys, the editors said, "Why don't you do it — get the donkeys, mine, smelt, and do action archaeology?" My answer: "If you pay for it, I'll do it."

The expedition, which was known as "Journey to the Copper Age," was a great opportunity for me to meet the two most important researchers working in Faynan — Jordanian archaeologist

THE BOOMER ARCHAEOLOGIST
• CHAPTER 30 •

Dr. Mohammad Najjar and German archaeometallurgist Professor Andreas Hauptmann. I sent them invitations by fax, and both promptly accepted. Thus began my long-term friendship and collaboration with Mohammad that continues until today. I arrived in the village of Dana, overlooking Faynan, with my Israeli colleagues, David Alon and Dodik Shoshani, and a Nat Geo team, including photographer Ken Garrett, an artist, a writer, and a photo editor. It was snowing! We were crammed into a Chevy Suburban driven by Israeli Bedouin Izzat Abu Rabia.

Crossing Jordan, 1997
Jordan-Israel Peace Treaty, October 26, 1994

I arranged to rent 10 donkeys and, in the morning, had not only the donkeys but also 10 Bedouins. Fortunately, the Nat Geo team had a briefcase full of $100 bills to distribute.

I planned the expedition so that after the 8-hour descent from the Edomite Plateau at Dana, we would camp out, and in the morning, mine for copper in the Wadi Khalid. The blue-green copper had been eroded out of the wadi and was spectacular. We used Chalcolithic flint and mining hammers to fill our saddlebags with ore. The next night we camped near Khirbat Hamra Ifdan, an Early Bronze Age copper factory I would soon be excavating.

The third day, we left the Wadi Faynan/Wadi Fidan gorge and crossed the Arabah Valley to the Israel border. Mohammad Najjar led the way, while Pierre coordinated with Jordanian military officers. Dodik used a primitive cell phone and coordinated with the Israeli army. We rode our donkeys across the Wilderness of Zin, where T.E. Lawrence and Leonard Wooley made a survey in 1914 of archaeological sites and, secretly, of the Ottoman Turkish military installations. Late one afternoon, one of the donkeys decided to take a "sand bath" and threw one of our team members off its back. The visit to the hospital slowed us down, and we arrived at Shiqmim 4 days later.

We pitched our tents at Shiqmim and instantly gathered ground stone tools to crush the copper ore from Faynan. Andreas had made clay-tipped bamboo blowpipes in Germany

Crossing Jordan, 1997
Jordan-Israel Peace Treaty, October 26, 1994

and carried them on his donkey. By nightfall, with charcoal from the Bedouin market in Beersheva, we successfully smelted copper according to the prehistoric methods we theorized. Our friendships were cemented by adventure, challenge, and action archaeology. Mohammad, Andreas, and I were ready for a new collaboration in Faynan. ✽

THE BOOMER ARCHAEOLOGIST

THOMAS EVAN LEVY

· CHAPTER 31 ·

Archaeometallurgy and Cyber-Archaeology in Jordan, 1999

THE BOOMER ARCHAEOLOGIST
• CHAPTER 31 •

By the fall of 1997, I had transported a 40-foot storage container filled with Israeli Army tents and excavation equipment from Israel to Jordan. I met the trucker at the border and guided him to the Bedouin village of Quarayqira, in the Faynan copper ore district. Ghazi Bisheh had kindly arranged for our team to have a 5-acre plot of land to be our long-term base of operations. That first season, I laid our camp out like the Hebrew letter "Chet" — like all Israeli army camps. As many of the tents had Hebrew names like "Commander's Tent," we raised some local eyebrows. I soon became good friends with Abu Shushi, the local paramount Sheikh (Chief) of the Amarin tribe, in whose neighborhood we resided. Abu Shushi liked to say I was "Sheikh Tom" when I came to Quarayqira. In the initial years, we had over 120 students and staff camping with us for periods of 2 ½ months. Pierre suggested I ask Queen Noor if I could borrow a Jordanian Air Force helicopter to take aerial photos of our sites. I was amazed when she generously said yes.

Ghazi suggested that being new to Jordan, I should take on a partner with experience in Faynan — Russ Adams. As Russ had worked for me at Shiqmim in 1987 as a supervisor, this seemed like a good idea. Mohammad Najjar joined the project as the Department of Antiquities partner. Andreas' pioneering archaeometallurgical work was carried out as a geologist sampling slag mounds and installations. Lacking was the social, economic, and historical context of ancient metallurgy in Faynan — perhaps the best-preserved ancient industrial landscape in the world. My open-air, large-scale excavation approach would help solve this. Those early years we concentrated on prehistory — Neolithic, Chalcolithic, and Early Bronze Age sites. In 1999, we excavated the late Pre-Pottery Neolithic (ca. 7500–7000 BCE) site of Tellet Ifdan at the entrance to Faynan in the Arabah Valley. While this was a pre-metal period, we found evidence of craft specialization in flint drills for bead manufacture with Faynan copper ores.

Archaeometallurgy & Cyber-Archaeology in Jordan, 1999

We also excavated the Early Bronze Age III/IV copper factory at Khirbat Hamra Ifdan (KHI). It is perhaps the best-preserved EBA metal factory in the Near East. We found thousands of objects related to copper production, including copper molds for casting pins, axes, and ingots. The crescent ingots were the same as those found in the Negev Desert at sites like Dever's Beer Ressisim, and our chemical analyses proved it. Each morning we would be in our 4x4 trucks, driving to these sites. It was incredibly exciting, as this part of Jordan was in many ways terra incognita for archaeologists.

TOM

MATT VINCENT

AT UMM AL-AMAD CAVE, HIGH ABOVE FAYNAN

From the time I was a teenager, I loved Arab culture. As a Jew, I have been committed to learning about Arab societies, and to meeting them as a member of my tribe. There are noted Jewish archaeologists who work in Syria and other

THE BOOMER ARCHAEOLOGIST
CHAPTER 31

Arab countries who proclaim they are Christian and hide their identity. With my last name, how could I hide it? I have always embraced my Judaism. It did not go unnoticed in Jordanian circles that I was the first "out of the closet" Jew to work in Jordan since Nelson Glueck. In 1997, one of the leaders of the British School of Archaeology in Amman proclaimed, "There is no way Tom Levy will get a license to dig in Jordan." From the day I first visited Jordan, I have been warmly welcomed by the Jordanian establishment and most of the Bedouin tribes in Faynan. The Jordanian Mukhabarat (Secret Police) knew everything about me.

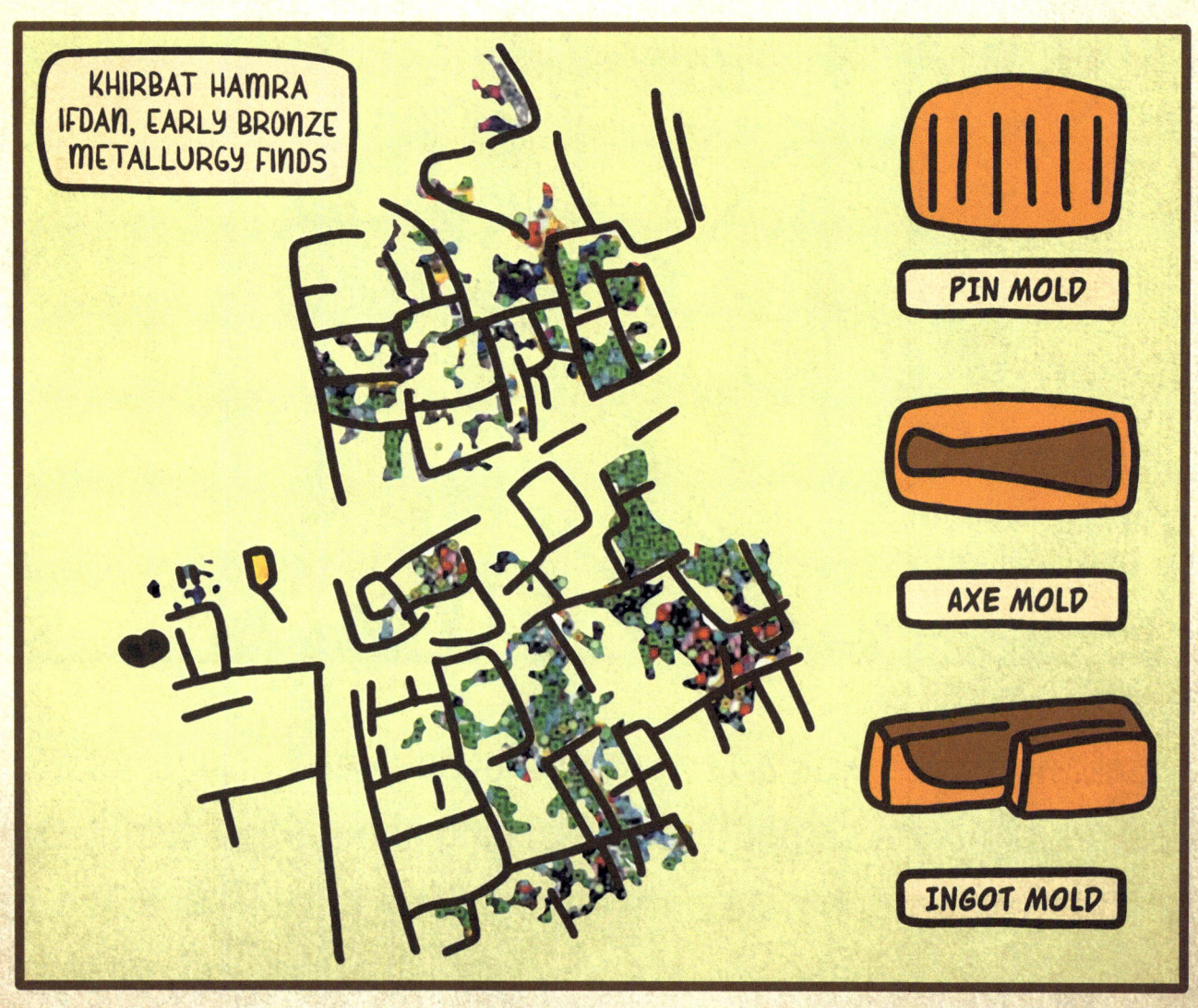

Archaeometallurgy & Cyber-Archaeology in Jordan, 1999

In 1999, I knew that any day the rug could be pulled out from under my research program, so it was best to embrace the Information Technology (IT) revolution happening in San Diego (and all over the world) and go completely digital on my excavations. That way, after each season, I would have the maximum amount of data, all recorded with X, Y, and Z (elevation) coordinates in a geo-spatial database where all data (photographs, digital models, typologies, etc.) could be linked. This is how my lab helped develop the field of "Digital/Cyber-Archaeology" in those early years. The map above shows the location of hundreds of EBA archaeometallurgical remains we discovered at KHI. By 2010, I was a Co-Principal Investigator (Co-PI) on a +$3 million NSF grant at UCSD to make archaeology a central part of a project called "Engineering for Cultural Heritage Diagnostics." Over the years, I have had some excellent PhD students who

THE BOOMER ARCHAEOLOGIST
CHAPTER 31

accompanied me on the Faynan expeditions, which often lasted for 2 ½ months and included living in a desert tent camp. Among these students were Yoav Arbel, Adolfo Muniz, Neil Smith, Erez Ben-Yosef, Aaron Gidding, Ian Jones, Kyle Knabb, Mark Beherec, Matt Howland, and Brady Liss.

By 2014, we perfected cyber-archaeology fieldwork in Jordan. The previous year I presented the model at a meeting of the American Academy of Arts and Sciences. My friend Chip Stanish, a New World archaeologist and member of the National Academy of Science, hosted me at the meeting. My model is based on 4 pillars: digital data capture, digital curation, analyses, and the dissemination of digital data over the Internet — with 3D visualization platforms, and old-fashioned peer-reviewed publications.

One of my favorite things about being a professor at a major research university has been the high quality of students I was able to mentor and work with. These students did not have the sense of entitlement that has recently crept into new cohorts of graduate students in the social sciences and humanities. Perhaps it was me. Occasionally, Yoav would say, "Graduate students either love to work with Tom Levy or hate it." Starting in 2015, the dropout rate of grad students in my lab rose exponentially, and I think this is true across the board at US research universities. That said, I'm especially proud of Erez, who has rapidly become a leader in Levantine archaeology, with a professorship at Tel Aviv University, state-of-the-art excavations in Israel's copper-rich Timna Valley, and an active archaeometallurgy laboratory.

My graduate students who worked with me in Jordan were excellent lab and field archaeologists. Like everyone, each faced their own challenges. By this I mean everything from being a Native American, Latino, gay, disabled, adopted, from a broken home, the child of Holocaust survivors, and more. This generation of students displayed resilience and a devotion to the archaeological endeavor that transcended their individual identities. For the most part, students and staff were united in their desire to be the best archaeological team possible. On these expeditions, our identity was the same — archaeologists.

Another one of my very talented graduate students is Neil Smith. When I think of my role in cyber-archaeology, if I may use a Biblical reference, it has been like a Moses figure trying to bring the field to the "Promised Land" of the 21st-century digital revolution. I think of Neil as my Joshua, who will truly bring the people into the promised land of cyber-archaeology with his archaeological and computer talents. ✡

THE BOOMER ARCHAEOLOGIST

THOMAS EVAN LEVY

• CHAPTER 32 •

Ethnoarchaeology in India, 2004–2007

THE BOOMER ARCHAEOLOGIST
• CHAPTER 32 •

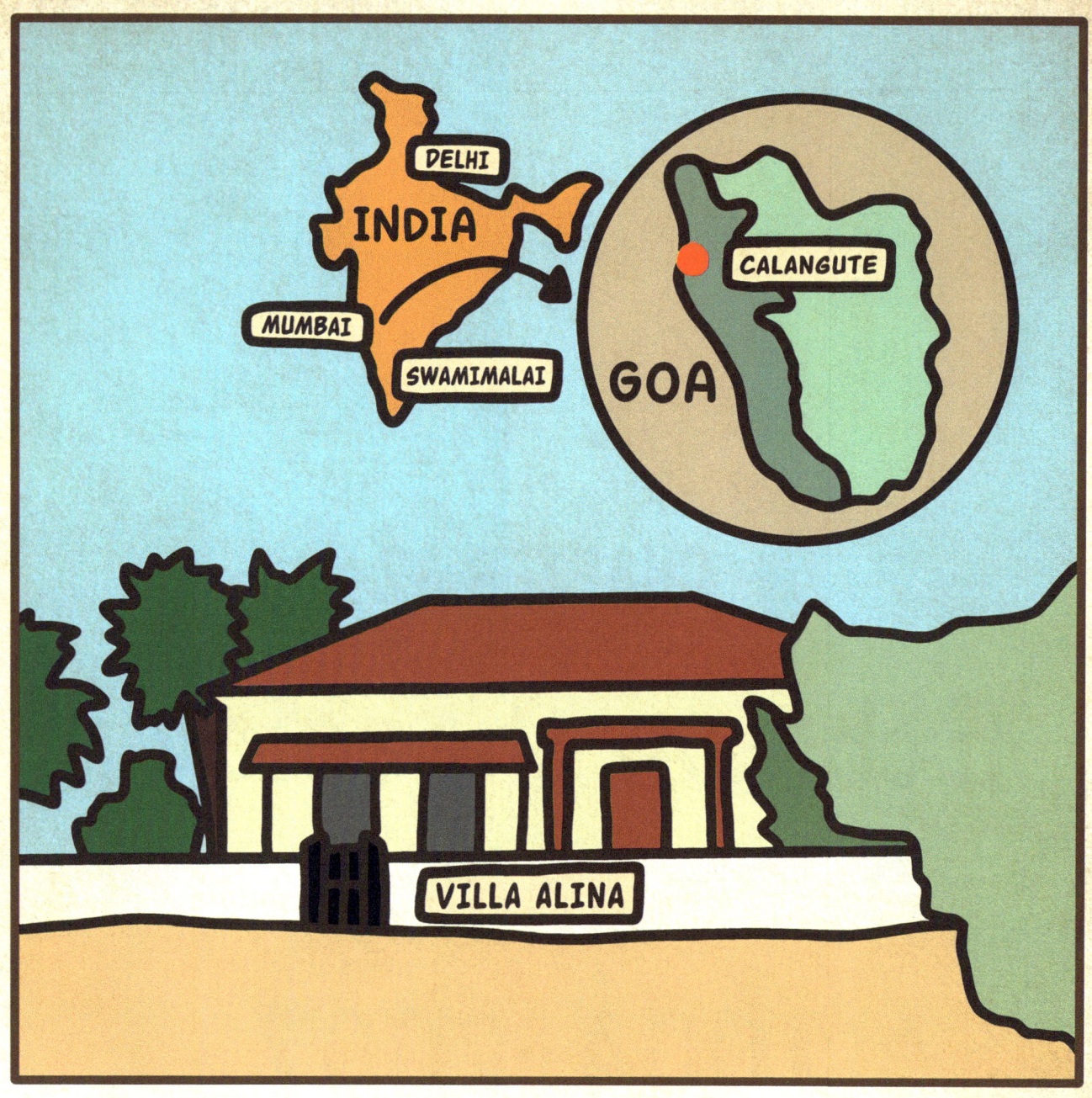

Goa is a tropical paradise and the ancestral home of Alina's family in India. Their roots go back hundreds of years in the village of Calangute. In the 1920s, Alirio's father built a house on the beach and named it after his wife — Villa Alina. Alina was named after her. My first visit to Goa with Alina was in 1982, and the family returns often. Alirio, Noemia, and their kids had to flee Tanzania in 1970 when the newly independent state turned against their Indian citizens.

Ethnoarchaeology in India, 2004–2007

As Asian refugees, they were proud to be in England. Having Villa Alina was a source of pride and "tribal roots" for the family. For years, I observed the itinerant blacksmiths from Maharashtra working on the streets in Calangute. I dreamt of doing an ethnoarchaeology project in India on traditional crafting, and my growing interest in archaeometallurgy led me to search for the makers of sacred Hindu temple bronzes.

In 2004, it was difficult to find information on where the iconic and sacred "Dancing Shiva" (Nataraja) bronze sculptures were

ALINA JUMPING OUT OF A 3-WHEELER TAXI DURING OUR SURVEY

THE BOOMER ARCHAEOLOGIST
CHAPTER 32

made in India. The Internet was not yet common. One day, I was lying in the hammock at Villa Alina reading the "Rough Guide to India." Suddenly I found a whole page devoted to hereditary bronze casting workshops in a village called Swamimalai in Tamil Nadu that produced the Nataraja! The following week, Alina and I made the 2-day trip to the village and started our survey of the +200 workshops. These craftsmen used a more than 1,000-year-old technique for bronze production based on the "lost-wax" method. Seeing this ancient crafting tradition up close and in action was a dream come true for an archaeologist.

During our second season of research in Swamimalai, we met the S. Devasenathipathy Sthapathy Sons in their workshop. They are the "rock stars" of traditional bronze crafting. Having made large statues for the Hare Krishna

movement, they have been featured in numerous books and film documentaries. Their great-great-grandfather won a craft prize from Queen Victoria. We thought they would have no time for us. However, the Sthapathy brothers became our dear friends and colleagues. When we published our book "Masters of Fire," we insisted they be co-authors with us. This was special because most cultural anthropologists never share authorship with the people they study.

GIANT WAX MODEL OF THE GODDESS PARVATI FOR A TEMPLE

While art historians, writers, and journalists had visited Swamimalai, we were the first to carry out a material culture ethnoarchaeology study of the hereditary bronze casters called "Sthapathys." Over 3 years, we recorded the "chaîne opératoire" (operational steps) of the ancient system from market forces to production, to each step in bronze making: carving a wax model, making the clay mold,

THE BOOMER ARCHAEOLOGIST
• CHAPTER 32 •

casting hot metal, breaking the mold, and finishing the icon. We also studied the genealogy of the Sthapathy community and ritual acts linked to the production of sacred bronzes.

One of the coolest things we discovered was the importance of metal recycling in the workshop. Walking in the back of the workshop one day, I saw a man washing the sediments. I asked Srikanda Sthapathy who he was, and I was told, "The mud washer. He comes every year for 2 weeks, digs up the casting floor near the furnaces, and cleans all our crucibles used to smelt and melt metal. By the time he leaves, we have over 100 kilos of recycled metal that we can recast into beautiful bronze icons." The implications of studying the Swamimalai workshops from an ethnoarchaeological perspective are huge for understanding ancient metal production in the archaeological record.

Ethnoarchaeology in India, 2004–2007

We learned so much from studying the hereditary bronze casters of South India. We helped the Sthapathy community tell their people's story. By identifying the chaîne opératoire for the lost-wax icon production, we produced a cross-cultural model to understand the enigmatic Chalcolithic prestige metal production in Israel. The Sthapathy recycling story helped us understand the organization of Iron Age (ca. 10th–9th c. BCE) copper production in Jordan. Finally, we were able to provide positive evidence on the health of this traditional craft, thanks to the success of the Indian diaspora around the world who purchase the sacred bronzes from Swamimalai. ✦

THE BOOMER ARCHAEOLOGIST

THOMAS EVAN LEVY

· CHAPTER 33 ·

Quest for Solomon's Mines, 2002–2014

THE BOOMER ARCHAEOLOGIST
· CHAPTER 33 ·

By the time Mohammad and I reached the age of 50, we were ready to excavate Iron Age copper production sites in Faynan. The Early Neolithic to Early Bronze Age periods were now behind us. The "Jewel in the Crown" for the Iron Age story was the site of Khirbat en-Nahas (KEN), first recorded by the Czech Orientalist Alois Musil in 1898 and then mapped by Nelson Glueck in 1934. Musil and Glueck have long been two of my heroes. KEN is a massive 25-acre copper smelting site with the largest Iron Age fortress in the deserts of southern Jordan, Israel, and Sinai. It has over 100 buildings protruding through the massive mounds of slag from ancient copper smelting activities.

In 2008, we published a high-impact paper in the Proceedings of the National Academy of Sciences (PNAS) — the third most important general science journal (after NATURE and SCIENCE). In it, we demonstrated that industrial-scale copper production at KEN was carried out in the 10th century BCE. We had over 100 radiocarbon dates to prove it! The pottery and other artifacts showed the people were local — not from Assyria or Egypt, so the archaeometallurgy and other finds supported aspects of the Hebrew Bible related to the time of King David and Solomon. It flew in the face of

THE BOOMER ARCHAEOLOGIST
• CHAPTER 33 •

Israel Finkelstein, my good friend, who wrote there were no kingdoms in Israel or Jordan (Edom) in the 10th c. BCE. National Geographic picked up our PNAS story and asked NOVA to make a documentary highlighting our work.

Prior to our work in the hyper-arid lowlands of Biblical Edom, where the copper ore is located, archaeologists focused on excavating in the highlands of Edom, where moister Mediterranean conditions would have existed. In 1940, Glueck published a book with a chapter devoted to "King Solomon's

Quest for Solomon's Mines, 2002–2014

Copper Mines." Based on his surveys, Glueck suggested Solomon's 10th c. BCE mines spread throughout the Wadi Arabah — centered in Faynan in the north and spreading 105 km south to Timna. From the early 1960s to 2002, Glueck's theory was debunked by "Biblical minimalists," who suggested the Iron Age in Edom only began ca. 600 BC, so any early stories in the Bible concerning the Hebrew kings, Edom, etc. were false. Mohammad and I were shocked when the radiocarbon dates from our excavations at KEN came back confirming Glueck's dating! When National Geographic/NOVA wanted to make the documentary, I insisted they pay around $100K toward our 2009 expedition. I wrote the script for the Jordan part and invited my friend and collaborator, Tom Higham, from the Oxford Radiocarbon Lab, to join us for the filming. Tom said it was the most exciting project he had ever been on.

THE BOOMER ARCHAEOLOGIST
• CHAPTER 33 •

Excavating KEN was a huge logistical challenge. The site was located along the remote and sandy Wadi al-Ghwayb. Up before sunrise, 10 4x4 pickup trucks would caravan, racing through the desert in the dark with me leading the way. From 2002 to 2009, each fall we camped in Quarayqira for 2.5 months and worked 6 days a week at KEN and other sites. It was cool to work on the documentary with my old Sheffield friend, Evan Hadingham, the senior science editor at NOVA.

Our scholarly legacy is our students. I'm very proud of my graduate students, and at the top of the list is Erez Ben-Yosef. I tasked Erez with being the archaeometallurgist for our work in Jordan for the 4 ⅓ years that he was my student. An Israeli, Erez was welcomed to work in Jordan under our UCSD umbrella. The deep 5x5-m probe into an industrial slag mound at KEN, over 6.5 m deep, was at the center of Erez's PhD study.

The excavations at KEN produced amazing evidence for a local Iron Age Edomite kingdom — a fortress, industrial metallurgy, elite buildings, and more, spanning the 10th–9th centuries BCE. It is possible that the early Israelite kings controlled KEN for a short period, but most evidence points to control by the Biblical Edomites. At the end of the 10th c. BCE, copper production was disrupted, and the fortress was decommissioned. The dating and a scarab we found at KHI suggested that the Egyptian Pharaoh Shoshenq I (Shishak) and his troops were the culprits. This was another intersection between the Bible, history, and archaeology.

THE BOOMER ARCHAEOLOGIST

THOMAS EVAN LEVY

· CHAPTER 34 ·

At-Risk World Heritage and the Oracle at Delphi

THE BOOMER ARCHAEOLOGIST
• CHAPTER 34 •

In 2013, I received an invitation from Professor Ioannis Liritzis at the University of the Aegean to participate in a digital archaeology conference in Delphi, Greece. We were at the end of our +$3 million NSF grant. I wanted to highlight our group's contribution to cyber-archaeology, so I arranged for a group of UCSD graduate students to accompany me to Greece to present our work from Jordan. Ioannis and I hit it off immediately. A physical scientist, Ioannis was trained in physics and is not an archaeologist. He grew up in Delphi and a neighboring village, Desfina, where he said there was an amazing Mycenaean site he would love to excavate. Late one evening during the conference, Ioannis said, "Let's take a drive. I want to show you something." Making our way slowly out of the Delphi village, we rolled up to the ice-cold Castalian Spring, where ancient Greek pilgrims would stop to quench their thirst before consulting the Delphic Oracle. I drank. "Now you will work with us here in Greece," Ioannis proclaimed.

THE BOOMER ARCHAEOLOGIST
• CHAPTER 34 •

From the beginning of my teaching career at UC San Diego, I have been a strong proponent of the undergraduate Faculty Mentor program. It allows the most talented students to work closely with a professor on original research. It prepares students for the professional world. Around 2010, I had 5 undergrads working with me on Jordanian material. They all presented their results at the prestigious undergrad research conference. After their stellar presentations, I congratulated them and said, "You represent the best of our meritocracy. That is why I chose you for the program." I was shocked by the comment of one of the students! Some of these students joined our cyber-archaeology field school in Delphi.

For 2 years, I ran the cyber-archaeology field school in Delphi with Ioannis and an impressive group of Greek scientists. My

graduate students Matt Howland and Brady Liss played a key part. It was awesome to be back in Greece, working. We did non-invasive recording of the monuments at ancient Delphi with a team from the Athena Research Center, led by George Pavlidis. We lived in lovely hotels in Delphi, and each night ate at a different restaurant so that Ioannis could share the wealth of having an American group in the village. Soon we were dancing every night to "Zorba the Greek" and my favorite Rembetika songs by Vamvakaris. Trying to get me in trouble, one of our anti-social American students complained to my administration that "Professor Levy was drunk and dancing on the tables." At the age of 62, I wished I could jump up on the tables. The best I could do is some simple Sirtaki and Zeibekiko steps. I never tired of spending time with friends in a taverna.

On August 18, 2015, the ISIS terrorists publicly beheaded Palmyra's Director of Antiquities, 81-year-old Khaled al-Asaad, when he refused to collaborate with the terrorists and tell them where he had hidden ancient artifacts from the Palmyra museum. This was just one example of the destruction of cultural heritage in the Middle East. This led me to apply to the University of California Office of the President Janet Napolitano Catalyst grant for "At Risk Cultural Heritage and the Digital Humanities." I received $1.3 million to bring 4 UC campuses together and carried out my part in Israel and Greece. The work in Greece was my first land and sea project.

THE BOOMER ARCHAEOLOGIST
• CHAPTER 34 •

ANCIENT PALYMYRA, SYRIA, 2015

At the time, the University of California cared about global issues, and our Catalyst award was proof of this. The site near Desfina is called "Kastrouli." In the early 1990s, grave robbers found an intriguing Dromos tomb there. Dating to the Late Helladic period, this was the time of the collapse of Mycenaean and other Late Bronze Age civilizations in the Eastern Mediterranean, ca. 1200 BCE. One of the tombs was open, and I thought it best to start there. Our students helped document it with our latest cyber-archaeology methods. After 2 days of digging, it was clear the thieves never penetrated the rich archaeological layers! Kastrouli was on the periphery of the Mycenaean civilization core, and yet we were finding gold and a rich assemblage of beautiful pottery in the tomb! How did Kastrouli provision itself? Trade? The answers could be found 5 km south in the Gulf of Corinth, which served as the maritime highway linking the Mycenaean together.

Thanks to Ioannis, I met Professors George Papatheodorou and Maria Geraga from the University of Patras. Their Laboratory of Marine Geology & Physical Oceanography may be the best shallow marine geophysics research team on the planet. Using the yacht "My Lady My Lord," we surveyed the sea floor of small bays near Late Helladic forts along the coast of the Bay of Antikyra in the Gulf of Corinth — close to Kastrouli. We cored underwater using scuba equipment with my colleague, Dick Norris, from Scripps. While the results related to Classical period Greece,

THE BOOMER ARCHAEOLOGIST
CHAPTER 34

we perfected underwater coring. Thanks to George, I was able to strengthen the third leg — shallow marine geophysics — of the new Scripps Center for Marine Archaeology (SCMA) toolbox. The other legs include sediment coring, paleoenvironmental reconstruction, underwater excavation, and photogrammetry. This is the approach I promoted as the co-director of SCMA with John Hildebrand. Around 2016, the university administration asked John (Scripps Institution of Oceanography) and me (Anthropology) to be the leaders of SCMA when the newly established center was in a major crisis. ✸

At-Risk World Heritage and the Oracle at Delphi

Lily and Tom on Phone Video Call

FALL IN LONDON

MY MOM AND I LOVED VISITING YOU AND AUNTY ALINA IN ANTIKYRA, WHEN YOU STARTED DOING MARINE ARCHAEOLOGY AT THE AGE OF 62 IN GREECE! WHY DID YOU LEAVE WORKING IN THE DESERT IN 2016?

TEMPERATE SAN DIEGO

I LOVE RESEARCH CHALLENGES. RATHER THAN REMAIN AN EXPERT IN THE CHALCOLITHIC PERIOD FOR MY CAREER, OVER THE YEARS I MOVED INTO OTHER PERIODS AND OTHER SUBFIELDS LIKE BIBLICAL/HISTORICAL ARCHAEOLOGY, ETHNOARCHAEOLOGY, AND CYBER-ARCHAEOLOGY. AFTER 40 YEARS OF FIELDWORK IN THE DESERTS OF THE HOLY LAND, IT WAS TIME TO COOL OFF! THE CHALLENGES OF MARINE ARCHAEOLOGY IN MY FIRST ARCHAEOLOGICAL LOVE, GREECE — AND MY HOMELAND, ISRAEL — WERE TOO TEMPTING TO JUMP IN AND NOT TRY SOMETHING COMPLETELY NEW.

THE BOOMER ARCHAEOLOGIST

THOMAS EVAN LEVY

· CHAPTER 35 ·

Underwater Archaeology in Israel

THE BOOMER ARCHAEOLOGIST
• CHAPTER 35 •

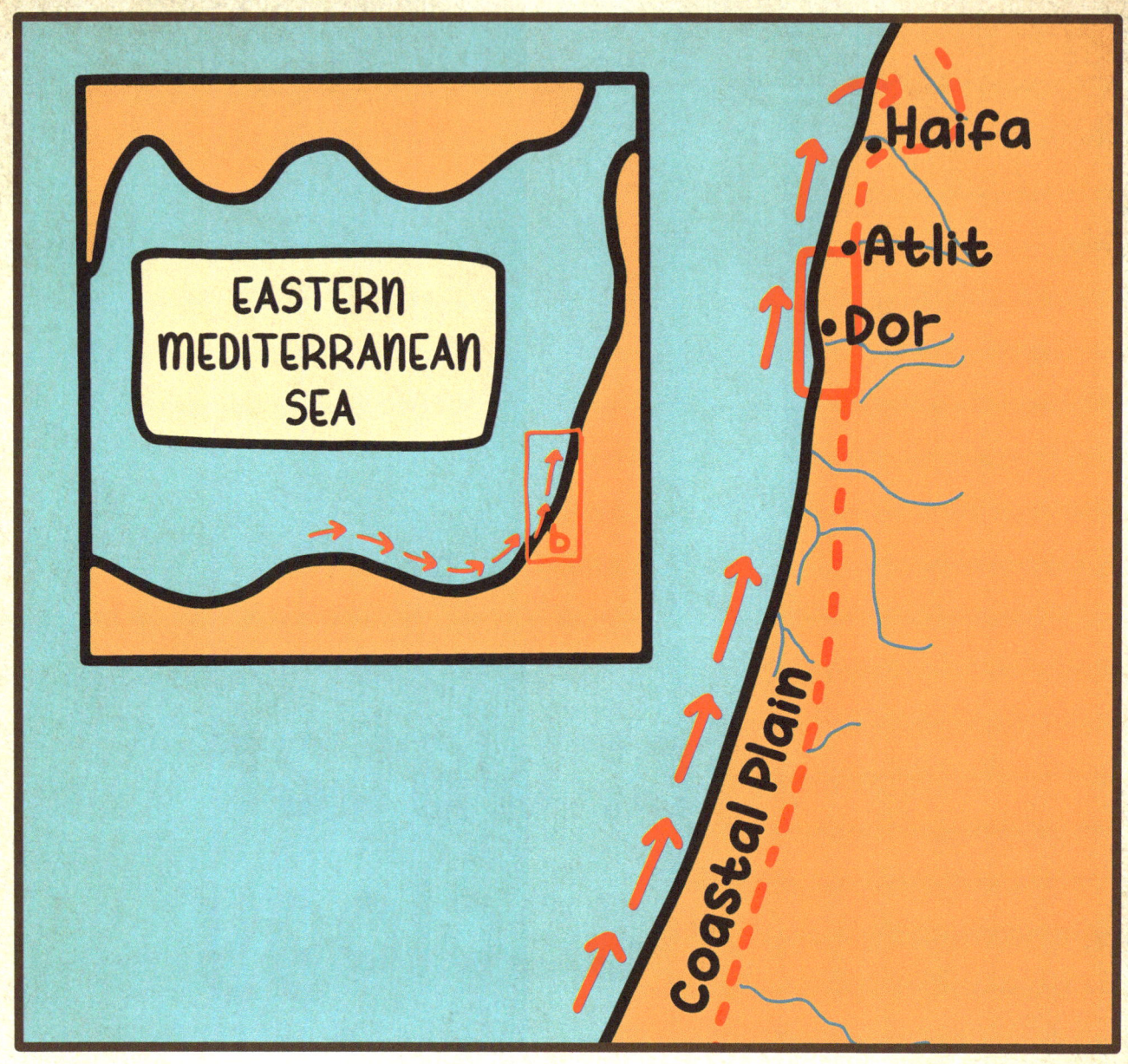

Having spent 40 years doing archaeology in the deserts of the Holy Land, I decided to cool off by shifting to underwater archaeology in 2015. Although I first qualified as a diver more than 50 years ago, in 1969, I fell in love with desert archaeology, and diving simply became too expensive an option. As co-director of SCMA, in 2016, I decided I had to be a qualified science diver. When I completed the Scripps 100-hour science diving course with Christian McDonald, I was the oldest person to pass it. But how to jump-start our program at an international level? We started with our Greek marine geophysics friends. Fortuitously, in 2017, I invited Assaf Yasur-Landau, a marine and land archaeologist from the University of Haifa, to teach at UCSD for the winter quarter. We talked and soon were planning a marine archaeology collaboration on Israel's Carmel coast. As the University of Haifa is one of the pioneers in underwater archaeology, Haifa was a perfect match for SCMA.

THE BOOMER ARCHAEOLOGIST
• CHAPTER 35 •

All those years in the Negev and Jordanian deserts kept me away from Israel's coastline. I always thought of it as flat, without much diversity. How wrong was I! There are numerous anchorages and sites spanning the past 10,000 years. Assaf suggested I join his research project in the small pocket bays around Tel Dor — an amazing ancient port city. Assaf had the permit to work in all the adjacent underwater areas. In the summer of 2017, I brought my new graduate student, Tony Tamberino, with me to do preliminary cyber-archaeology surveys around the site in preparation for our future work. The following summer we, had our first joint Haifa-UCSD underwater archaeology field school.

Although I worked many years in Jordan, each year I traveled to Israel before or after our dig to see friends

and keep up with Israeli archaeology. It is exciting to cross from Jordan to Israel over the Allenby (King Hussein) Bridge. With marine archaeology, I'm back to my roots in Israel. Thanks to adopting Ben and Gil, Alina and I are fluent in Hebrew, which makes each visit invigorating, as I'm re-immersed in our shared Israeli and Middle Eastern culture. Working together with the Scripps science diving officers Christian McDonald and Rich Walsh, and their University of Haifa counterparts — Amir Yurman and Mosheko Bahar (ex-Israeli Navy Seals) — made the caliber of our work outstanding.

The year 2018 marked the beginning of a beautiful Haifa-San Diego relationship. As part of our joint underwater archaeology field school, Haifa built a cool barge to carry a diesel-water-pump dredge system for shallow excavations, and UCSD developed new underwater photogrammetry workflows for more accurate recording. By 2020, I had secured a 3-year, +$1.3 million grant from the Koret Foundation's US-Israel Bridge-Building Initiative to enable UCSD SCMA to work closely with the Leon Recanati Institute for Maritime Studies.

The third pillar of my SCMA approach to marine archaeology came together in 2017, when I met Gilad Shtienberg on the beach at Dor. After working in Greece, Dick Norris and I wanted to perfect a strategy for coring in the near coastal zone. I was impressed by Gilad and invited him to help plan a coring expedition while we were digging with Assaf at Dor. Gilad's tool of choice was the Geoprobe — a small tractor-driven machine that uses dynamic percussion force to pound in plastic core barrels into the coast to obtain sediment cores.

By 2019, I had invited Gilad to be my postdoc at our UCSD SCMA sedimentology lab. At a seminar one day, we were highly skeptical of archaeologists who said they found evidence of tsunamis. A few days later, Gilad called me excitedly: "We found clear evidence of a Neolithic tsunami at Dor!" To date, this is the oldest recorded tsunami in the Eastern Mediterranean. We published it in the prestigious journal — PLOS One.

As of 2021, antisemitism has been raising its ugly head at elite American universities. I experienced this during the 2021 Gaza war, when the UCSD Graduate and Professional

THE BOOMER ARCHAEOLOGIST
° CHAPTER 35 °

Association targeted our Koret Israel project — making a resolution on June 4 to end all UCSD-University of Haifa collaboration. Fortunately, some brave Jewish and Israeli graduate students got the motion tabled. Unfortunately, the hate against Jews and Israel has spread in the US system. ✡

Underwater Archaeology in Israel

Lily and Uncle Tom on Computer Video Call

LONDON

UNCLE TOM, HOW DO YOU EXPLAIN THE RISE OF RAMPANT ANTISEMITISM AND ANTI-ISRAEL FEELING AND ACTIVITIES ON AMERICAN ELITE UNIVERSITY CAMPUSES?

SAN DIEGO

MY FRIEND AND FELLOW ARCHAEOLOGIST, ALEX JOFFE, WHO IS THE EDITOR OF THE BDS (BOYCOTT, DIVESTMENT, SANCTIONS) MONITOR, FOR "SCHOLARS FOR PEACE IN THE MIDDLE EAST" FOLLOWS THIS CLOSELY. ACCORDING TO ALEX, "THE QUESTION OF ANTISEMITISM HAS NOTHING TO DO WITH JEWS OR ISRAEL AND EVERYTHING TO DO WITH THE ANTISEMITE'S SEARCH FOR MEANING AND CERTAINTY. ON CAMPUSES WHERE TRADITION AND BEAUTY WERE DESTROYED, ANTISEMITISM IS THE BENEFICIARY." I'VE SEEN MANY STUDENTS WHO COME FROM BROKEN FAMILIES, WHO HAVE NO RELIGION, OR IDENTITY, BECOME BRAINWASHED BY PROFESSORS WHO PEDDLE THE OPPRESSED/OPPRESSOR MODEL OF MARXISM ON THEM. FOR 2 THOUSAND YEARS, UNHAPPY PEOPLE AROUND THE WORLD HAVE TARGETED THE JEWS WITH HATRED IN THEIR BIZARRE SEARCH FOR MEANING.

THE BOOMER ARCHAEOLOGIST

THOMAS EVAN LEVY

• CHAPTER 36 •

The Collapse of Civilizations

THE BOOMER ARCHAEOLOGIST
• CHAPTER 36 •

Since I began to teach at UCSD in 1992, my courses have dealt with the collapse of civilizations. There is always a beginning, a middle, and an end to these remarkable institutions. However, I never thought I would see it happen in my own lifetime! On September 11 (9/11), 2001, the phone rang. It was my mother-in-law Noemia. I thought she called to wish me happy birthday. All she said was, "Tom, turn on the TV." It soon became clear that terrorists were responsible for the attack on the World Trade Center in New York, the Pentagon outside

The Collapse of Civilizations

DC, and another target probably intended to hit the White House — all key symbols of American power and civilization. How could the US Intelligence Community (IC) miss detecting the terrorists' plans? American complacency? A year later, our team was in Jordan for the first excavations at KEN. Our project studied what happened after the collapse of the Late Bronze Age civilizations in Jordan, in the following Iron Age (ca. 1200–500 BCE). I went to our local liquor store in Amman to buy beer for the expedition. At the cash register, the clerk asked, "Wanna buy something really cool?" He pulled out a box of Zippo lighters celebrating 9/11. I declined the offer.

9/11 marked the first time I realized just how fragile our United States democracy is. When America was waging the Vietnam War in the '60s and early '70s, it was far away from our shores, and I didn't see the USA under threat then. Hence my decision in 1971 to stay in Israel and wait to see if I would be selected in the draft lottery. Had I been drafted, I would have stayed on in Israel. But 9/11 was different. Scholars have suggested 5 primary causes for the collapse of civilizations: 1) major episodes of climate change; 2) social crises due to mass migrations and pandemics; 3) dramatic advances in methods of transport; 4) warfare; and 5) the inability of humans to adapt to crises, such as lack of social resilience and poor elite leadership in those civilizations. Punctuated societal change stimulated by any

THE BOOMER ARCHAEOLOGIST
• CHAPTER 36 •

or all of these variables can lead to the collapse of civilization. Writing my memoir during the COVID-19 pandemic, and the failure of US institutions and leadership to respond to rapid change, leads me to ask if American civilization — as an exceptional nation — is now in a process of collapse? I didn't want to see this happening to us on my watch...

Sometime around the 2010s, I began to notice how identity politics became one of the most important organizing principles

of not only our students but also the UC San Diego faculty. This is where people of a particular race, religion, or social background create exclusive political alliances. It's about the "Privileged" vs. the "Oppressed" and the need to resist. Amy Chua, in her book "Political Tribes" (2018), calls America a supergroup — a tribe of tribes, with citizenship open equally to anyone born on US soil or those who immigrate and become US citizens — no matter their ancestry. Unfortunately, Intersectionality and Critical Race Theory (CRT) are all working together to destroy the exceptional American supergroup; and our educational institutions are failing to keep the supergroup going.

Over the past decade, our campus administration went to great lengths to create "safe spaces" for students from different ethnic/racial groups. The downside of this was the

THE BOOMER ARCHAEOLOGIST
· CHAPTER 36 ·

creation of more, not less, student anxiety and isolation. I went back online to review the Intersectionality model to see how these coalitions are structured. I discovered that the new model erases Jews! Jews practically invented the notion of "Intersectionality," exemplified by our leaders such as the great Rabbi Abraham Joshua Heschel. In fact, the progressive movement in America has usurped so much from Jewish history. Terms like "genocide," "exodus," and "ghetto," came out of the earlier Jewish experience but are now being forgotten.

The Collapse of Civilizations

Back in 2015, with the killings of journalists at Charlie Hebdo and a kosher market in Paris, journalists wrote: "If France is not safe for Jews, then the very future of Europe — and indeed the civilized world — is in real danger." History has shown that Jews are the proverbial canary in a coal mine. The canaries in a mine die before humans are aware of the presence of untraceable poisonous gases — their death is a warning of impending disaster. So too is the state of Jews in their respective societies a test for the safety of the society at large. If you revisit Kimberlé Crenshaw's models of Intersectionality today, it is disturbing to see that Jews have been erased from the oppressed due to antisemitism. The rise of antisemitism in the USA reflects this process. On US college campuses, this manifests itself in a hatred of Israel. When societies target their Jews, this is another indicator of societal collapse. Let's remember Martin

THE BOOMER ARCHAEOLOGIST
• CHAPTER 36 •

Niemöller, a Lutheran minister and early Nazi supporter who was later imprisoned for opposing Hitler's regime, who said, "First they came for the socialists, and I did not speak out — because I was not a socialist. Then they came for the trade unionists, and I did not speak out — because I was not a trade unionist. Then they came for the Jews, and I did not speak out — because I was not a Jew. Then they came for me — and there was no one left to speak for me."

The collapse of American prowess as a leader in social science and humanities can be seen in academic departments across the USA. The meritocracy that made our universities great in these fields is dead. My department is a microcosm of this process. In the old days, excellence was measured by peer-reviewed publications, successful grant applications, and placement of graduates. Today, it is based on identity politics and virtue signaling, op-ed pieces, and the display of crocodile tears on behalf of "the oppressed," while faculty enjoy large salaries and can use video conferencing to teach, never having to be on campus. This is emblematic of the failure of American institutions across the country and the collapse of the American supergroup. Is there a way out of this debacle? ✡

THE BOOMER ARCHAEOLOGIST

THOMAS EVAN LEVY

• EPILOGUE •

Gratitude

THE BOOMER ARCHAEOLOGIST
· EPILOGUE ·

I want to end my memoir on a positive note, and the best way to do that is through gratitude. I have been blessed with a passion for archaeology since the age of 12, when anthropologist Count Taylor became a dear friend of our family. Anthropology seemed like a key for understanding people and the tapestry of cultures and ethnic groups that I

Gratitude

was being exposed to as I grew up. Growing up in California, I soon realized that at my young age, while I could not practice cultural anthropology, I could immediately get involved with archaeology — one of the four subfields of anthropology. From then on, with the exception of working in the cowsheds of Israel, I have never done any other jobs except archaeology. I gravitated to the Eastern Mediterranean, and especially Israel, for my work. Israel and the Southern Levant are at the crossroads of world culture, and I've been fortunate to focus my work where my tribal roots are.

I'm especially grateful for having my father's unconditional love as I grew up into my early adulthood. As I reflected early on in this memoir, my father was selfless. My father was a very unique individual — a rare breed in this materialistic world, especially in the USA where I grew up. Dad taught me to respect everyone who worked hard, no matter what their station in life or identity. Dad encouraged me to dream in ways that he never could, to be proud of our Jewish identity, to defend our right to self-determination, and to be respectful of all others. At the time of writing this memoir, my mother was 97 years old; I'm grateful to have had her in my life.

I'm most grateful for meeting Alina when we were young, having her by my side as we both grew together over the years, and for our long, meaningful, and loving marriage.

THE BOOMER ARCHAEOLOGIST
• EPILOGUE •

We work on it. I'm grateful that Alina challenges me to be a better and more thoughtful person each and every day. In Yiddish, Alina is my "B'Shert" — soulmate, an ideal predestined marriage partner. To my young readers, this is definitely old school and something you should strive for.

Being born into the Jewish tribe has given me a beautiful anchor to help navigate life. I am grateful to have been born at a time when Israel was no longer a dream but a

Gratitude

reality, and for having had the opportunity to participate in the Israel experiment to the fullest. The vibrancy, resilience, and light that emanate from Israel continue to be a daily inspiration for me.

I was privileged to have been born in California and the USA. While the notion of privilege is demonized in US society today, the truth is that every one of us born in this country, or immigrated here, is privileged if compared to every other country on the planet. Americans can reinvent themselves in ways that people in other countries cannot. It is disingenuous not to acknowledge our good fortune. Being part of the universal tapestry of human cultures is equally important for me.

THE BOOMER ARCHAEOLOGIST
• EPILOGUE •

Family — I'm grateful for our sons Ben and Gil. B and G have added so much to my life's adventure with Alina. Our life in Israel, where children are such an important part of the fabric of life, would not have been the same without Ben and Gil. For over 40 years, Alina's family, with their roots in India, have been a constant source of love and inspiration for me. When visiting my mother-in-law Noemia in London or Goa, she always pampered me with a welcoming plate of samosas. These treats were accompanied by significant questions from both Noemia and Alirio about what my latest research and adventures were all about. They were genuinely interested in what I was doing, and I deeply miss those moments. I would be remiss not to mention the incredible Boxer dogs in my life! Starting when I was a baby with Rex at my side, and then

Gratitude

Sandy in Israel — and our early years in the USA with Alina, me, and the boys — and finally, Shula.

Retirement as a professor is now a reality for me. I'm grateful to my graduate students who have accompanied me on so many adventures and research described here. After spending 40 years excavating and surveying in the deserts of Israel and Jordan, during the past decade, I'm grateful for being able to have shifted to marine archaeology in the

THE BOOMER ARCHAEOLOGIST
• EPILOGUE •

Eastern Mediterranean. This is thanks to my dear friends and colleagues in Israel, Jordan, and Greece; and the support of my patrons, such as the late Norma Kershaw, whom I met so long ago at the Biblical site of Tel Gezer in 1971, when I was 17 and Norma was at 47. By creating the Kershaw Chair in the Archaeology of Ancient Israel and Neighboring Lands, Norma and Rube wanted to support me, but more importantly ensure that this field be taught and researched in perpetuity at UCSD. At the time of writing this memoir, it is not clear if the faculty at my former department will keep to the terms of this endowment. While I'm disturbed by the "woke" trend in elite American research universities, I am very grateful for having been privileged to work at UC San Diego as a professor for 30 years. The opportunities for research, innovation, and exploration were phenomenal at this educational jewel on the Pacific Ocean.

Gratitude

Lily and Uncle Tom on Phone Call

LILY IN BALMY UK

Uncle Tom, it's so cool that you end your story on positive vibes. One last question, how were your final days at the university?

UNCLE TOM IN HOT BORREGO SPRINGS

To be honest, they weren't great. In their quest to "decolonize" anthropology, my colleagues could not appreciate the need for archaeological collections. They were busy ferreting out Native American artifacts on our campus to repatriate. There were talks about investigating artifacts from other regions without understanding how different countries and cultures view issues of patrimony. The government of Jordan had given me and UCSD a permanent loan of over 35 tons of artifacts from our work in Faynan! Many PhDs and scholarly works came of this collection! In the months before I retired, the Jordanian government gave me permission to move the collection to La Sierra University — a 2-hour drive from La Jolla. My Seventh Day Adventist brothers and sisters at La Sierra were thrilled to receive the collection that is now called the "Tom Levy and Mohammad Najjar Edom, Jordan Archaeological Collection," and will be part of their new museum. Lily, there is more, but let's leave it at that.

THE BOOMER ARCHAEOLOGIST

THOMAS EVAN LEVY

• PHOTO STORY 1 •

Shiqmim

The Rise of Social Inequality, ca. 4500–3600 BCE

https://www.academia.edu/42642430/Levy_T_E_2003_Cult_Metallurgy_and_Rank_Societies_Chalcolithic_Period_ca_4500_3500_BCE_In_The_Archaeology_of_Society_in_the_Holy_Land_edited_by_T_E_Levy_pp_226_244_Continuum

THE BOOMER ARCHAEOLOGIST
• PHOTO STORY 1 •

Lunch during Shiqmim survey, 1977

The survey along the ca. 120 km long Wadi Beersheva-Wadi Gaza revealed one of the earliest regional polities in the Southern Levant. During the Chalcolithic period, there were 4 clusters of integrated settlements along the wadi system, with one of the largest at Shiqmim.

Tom inside underground storage silos, 1989

The discovery of extensive networks of underground room and tunnel complexes at Shiqmim highlights the importance of storage for the staple goods (crops) that helped fuel the chiefdom economy.

Yoav Arbel in underground room, 1989

The enigmatic subterranean room complexes are like human "Ant Farms." An average underground system could include 9 or 10 rooms of different sizes that were connected by tunnels. They were used for storage, defense, human burial, and adaptation to desert conditions. It was extremely dangerous to excavate these subterranean room complexes.

Shiqmim
The Rise of Social Inequality, ca. 4500–3600 BCE

Helicopter view of Shiqmim camp and dig, 1987

The Phase 2 excavations (1987–89, 1993) at Shiqmim focused on exploring the evolution of the Beersheva Valley Chalcolithic chiefdom. The deep trenches helped reveal networks of underground rooms and tunnels.

Prestige and other metal works played an important role in the wealth finance system that fueled the Shiqmim chiefdom. Chiefs controlled metallurgy and the distribution of these precious items. Similar beautifully preserved objects were found in the "Cave of the Treasure" in the 1960s.

Corroded copper standard with asphalt

Tom gives tour to IDF soldiers at the cemetery, 1982

In 1979, we discovered the first Chalcolithic cemetery in the Northern Negev. It is extensive, over 800 m in length and adjacent to the Shiqmim village. It highlights the notion of local burial and territoriality in the Beersheva Valley chiefdom.

THE BOOMER ARCHAEOLOGIST

THOMAS EVAN LEVY

• PHOTO STORY 2 •
Gilat

Earliest Temples in the Holy Land, ca. 4500–3600 BCE

https://www.academia.edu/43214689/2006_Archaeology_Anthropology_and_Cult_Exploring_Religion_in_Formative_Middle_Range_Societies_In_Archaeology_Anthropology_and_Cult_The_Sanctuary_at_Gilat_Israel

THE BOOMER ARCHAEOLOGIST
◦ PHOTO STORY 2 ◦

Sacred Objects from Gilat

The oldest temples in the Middle East date to the Pre-Pottery Neolithic period in Turkey, ca. 9500–8000 BCE. However, in the Holy Land, temples first appeared during the Chalcolithic period, and Gilat is one of the 3 known examples. David Alon and I excavated Gilat between 1976 and 1992. We discovered the "Holy of Holies" and found the now-famous "Gilat woman with churn," "Ram with cornet vessels," stone violin figurines, and more. The Woman and Ram reflect the "Secondary Products Revolution" — a Chalcolithic happening. (Photo by K. Garett)

Extensive remains of ritual acts were found in each occupation stratum at the Gilat Chalcolithic temple. This included the burial of dogs. The example shown here was carefully interred with a unique ceramic vessel at its feet. Our archaeozoologist Caroline Grigson showed that during its lifetime, this special dog had broken its leg and then carefully nurtured back to good health.

Tom examines dog burial and grave offering

Gilat pottery and Bedouin woman churning

The "Secondary Products Revolution" refers to when animal milk, wool, hair, and traction — rather than meat — were first intensively exploited. Earlier, animals were only kept for their meat. The ancient ceramic milk churn on the left served the same function as the skin one used by the Bedouin woman on the right — to make products like yogurt and cheese. Sophisticated pastoralism and the Mediterranean diet crystallized during the Chalcolithic. This included domesticated dates and olives. (Photo by K. Garett)

Gilat
Earliest Temples the Holy Land ca. 4500-3600 BCE

Sample of Gilat's violin shape stone figurines

My friend, Chip Stanish, wrote an important book ("The Evolution of Human Co-operation") showing how ritual and religion, rather than state-sponsored coercion, can create complex societies — like chiefdoms. Ritual practices create unique rules of behavior for organizing society. Gilat has a wealth of such evidence, including the widespread distribution of beautiful violin-shaped figurines seen here, which were made of stones from different regions of the Holy Land, torpedo-shaped ceramic vessels (previous page) made in different regions and brought to Gilat as offerings with olive oil, and more that reflect ritual acts. (Photo by K. Garett)

Excavating a primary burial at the Gilat temple

Over 85 human burials were found in the different strata associated with the Gilat temple complex. Being buried in and around the sanctuary complex may reflect the ancient residents of Gilat or pilgrims to the ritual center.

Cache of 4 complete ostrich eggs

The magisterial work "Treasures of Darkness" by Thorkild Jacobsen shows how, during the origins of ancient Near Eastern religion in the 4th millennium BCE, the gods were embodiments of economically important products. Similarly, our work at Gilat shows widespread ritual acts connected to the importance of secondary animal products (milk, wool, hair, traction) and human fertility. They stimulated the rise of one of the earliest temples in the Southern Levant. The Gilat ostrich egg cache was part of a foundation deposit for the main temple plaza (Stratum IIC). Located at the entry to the rich Negev coastal plain grazing lands, Gilat emerged as a ritual center for Chalcolithic societies concerned with pastoralism.

THE BOOMER ARCHAEOLOGIST

THOMAS EVAN LEVY

• PHOTO STORY 3 •

Copper Trail

Journey to the Copper Age Action Archaeology, 1997

THE BOOMER ARCHAEOLOGIST
• PHOTO STORY 3 •

Tom negotiates for donkeys with local Bedouin in Dana village

In March 1997, the National Geographic Society asked me to organize an "action or experimental archaeology" project to reconstruct how Chalcolithic people mined copper ore in Jordan's Faynan region, transported it to Israel's Beersheva Valley, and smelted it into copper metal. This would be the first joint project involving Jordanian, Israeli, American, and German researchers. We began the journey high up on the Edom plateau overlooking the copper ore region — and it was snowing! An article appeared in the 1999 issue of National Geographic Magazine.

The donkey caravan involved a 10-day archaeological journey with Jordanian archaeologist Mohammad Najjar; German archaeometallurgist Andreas Hauptmann; Israeli researchers David Alon, Dodik Shoshani, and Avner Goren; and Americans Pierre Bikai and Tom Levy. The expedition took place 3 years after the signing of the Israel-Jordan peace treaty so this was both an important and optimistic project. The text of the National Geographic article was good, however, it did not highlight the significance of this international expedition after more than 45 years of war.

Donkey caravan takes a break in Wadi Dana, Jordan

Tom removes baby goat from Chalcolithic mine

The 2 main copper ore sources in the Southern Levant are in the Arabah Valley that separates modern Israel and Jordan. In the north, closest to the Beersheva Valley is Faynan — about a 150 km donkey-ride away. In the south is Timna. Lead isotope and chemical studies of copper metal and ores found at the Beersheva Chalcolithic sites, like Shiqmim, show the source to be Faynan. Chalcolithic mines, like the one from Wadi Khalid shown here, exploited copper minerals such as malachite.

Copper Trail
Journey to the Copper Age Action Archaeology, 1997

Mining copper in Wadi Khalid, Jordan

After the 6-hour descent from the plateau, we reached the Wadi Khalid with our donkeys. Andreas Hauptmann had found a number of Chalcolithic mines in this area. Beautiful deposits of bright green malachite still glistened in the wadi section. This was the perfect place to begin mining ore — first with stone hammers, but then with modern mining hammers as we needed to establish our evening camp. We wanted to fill our saddlebags with copper ore for transport across the desert to the Wadi Beersheva and the ancient Shiqmim Village.

Evening view of copper smelting and subterranean rooms at Shiqmim

It took 7 days to ride our donkeys to Shiqmim. Bureaucratic delays from the Jordanian and Israeli armies slowed up our travel. No doubt, different kinds of "red tape" were also faced by ancient travelers. On a good day, we could average 30 km. By our first evening at Shiqmim, we had been conducting smelting experiments for over 6 hours.

Tom, Andreas Hauptmann, and Avner Goren smelting copper ore at Shiqmim

After hours of trial and error, we discovered that to successfully smelt 10 grams of pure copper, it took 30–45 minutes of a constant stream of air from our blowpipes. The average weight of a pure Chalcolithic copper chisel/axe is about 370 grams. Thus, it would take from 18 ½–28 hours to smelt enough pure copper for a chisel/axe. The ratio of copper chisel/axe to those made of flint is 1:250, meaning these objects were very rare and required a huge amount of labor (add transport time). Although we classify these items as "tools," they were probably highly valued in the wealth-based Chalcolithic chiefdom economy — just like the prestige alloyed copper metal objects made famous from their discoveries in the "Cave of the Treasure."

All photos by K. Garrett

THE BOOMER ARCHAEOLOGIST

THOMAS EVAN LEVY

• PHOTO STORY 4 •
The Edom Lowlands Regional Archaeology Project (ELRAP), Jordan

Copper and the Rise of a Biblical Iron Age Kingdom, 10th–9th Centuries BCE

THE BOOMER ARCHAEOLOGIST
· PHOTO STORY 4 ·

Balloon view of Khirbat en-Nahas (KEN) copper factory; for scale, see pickup truck at bottom right

After the collapse of Bronze Age civilizations in the Eastern Mediterranean (ca. 1200 BCE), the island of Cyprus ceased to be the primary supplier of copper in the region. This power vacuum enabled the Faynan region to become a major copper producer in the following Iron Age. We carried out extensive excavations at KEN, a massive +25-acre copper factory. As seen here, the site is covered in extensive black copper slag. Note: A = Fortress gatehouse, R = Elite building, and M = Slag mound excavation.

In Area M, our team sampled one of the numerous slag mounds visible on the surface of KEN. The slag (waste remains from smelting copper ore) deposits extended for over 6 m in depth. Unprecedented radiocarbon dating of the layers of slag demonstrated industrial-scale copper production was rapid at KEN, and took place mostly over 2 centuries — in the 10th and 9th centuries BCE. This corresponds with the kingdoms of Israel, Judah, and Edom mentioned in the Hebrew Bible (Old Testament).

Area M slag mound excavation

Tom samples for radiocarbon dating at KEN; Shosheng I/Shishak scarab found in Faynan

This is the second epigraphic artifact found in the Holy Land with the name of the 10th c. BCE Pharaoh Shishak mentioned in the Bible (I Kings 14:25).

High-precision radiocarbon dating of the slag mound in Area M, coupled with those in the fortress and monumental building, demonstrated local kingdom or state-level control of metallurgy during the 10th and 9th c. BCE. No evidence of the Assyrian Empire was found. Researchers such as Israel Finkelstein argued there were no kingdoms (thus no complex societies led by David, Solomon, and the Edomites) in the 10th c. BCE Southern Levant. Our data published in PNAS and a 2-volume final monograph demonstrated that local kingdoms mentioned in the Hebrew Bible — not the Assyrians — controlled industrial copper production during that period.

https://doi.org/10.1073/pnas.0804950105

The Edom Lowlands Regional Archaeology Project (ELRAP), Jordan
Copper and the Rise of a Biblical Iron Age Kingdom, 10th-9th century BCE

Monumental Building at KEN

The monumental 2-storey 10th c. BCE building in Area R measures 14.75 m x 13.16 m and contains a courtyard surrounded by 6 rooms. It has a well-built entrance with 2 small protruding walls, each ca. 2 m in length. The preservation was remarkable, with walls standing over 2 m in height. An extensive perimeter wall, 32.6 m long x 22.3 m wide, protected the building, which had a stone "throne" built on the side of the entrance. Probably the residence of an elite, iron tools, fine Midianite pottery and other prestige objects were found here.

This reconstructed ceramic vessel (approx. 30 cm high) was found next to the monumental building in Area R. The decoration on this pot reflects the north Arabian Midianite style common in the 10th c. BCE. This vessel and others found at KEN point to connections between Jordan's Edom region and the Iron Age tribal area of Midian. Some scholars suggest the Midianites, known from the Hebrew Bible (cf. Exodus 18:1-27), were metallurgical specialists who worked at Timna and other sites in the Wadi Araba that separates modern Israel and Jordan.

"Midianite" pottery vessel from elite building

Tom and Mohammad hold Explorers Club flag with team, Faynan

The ELRAP expeditions helped pioneer the new field of cyber-archaeology: the integration of the latest developments in computer science, engineering, the natural sciences, and archaeology. ELRAP and the excavations at KEN used some of the first "paperless" recording systems for archaeology. The workflow included digital data collection, curation, analyses, and dissemination over the internet, with 3D visualization platforms and traditional peer-reviewed publications.

https://www.amacad.org/news/cyber-archaeology-and-world-cultural-heritage-insights-holy-land

THE BOOMER ARCHAEOLOGIST

THOMAS EVAN LEVY

• PHOTO STORY 5 •

Ethnoarchaeology

The Hereditary Bronze Casters of South India

THE BOOMER ARCHAEOLOGIST
• PHOTO STORY 5 •

The Sthapathy brothers, Tom and Alina in their bronze-casting workshop

Ethnoarchaeology refers to the study of contemporary people using the research questions and tools of archaeologists. Data from the study of living traditional societies can provide potent comparative models for achaeology. From 2004 to 2007, Alina and I began a 3-year project to study the traditional "lost-wax" bronze technology and culture of the hereditary bronze casting community known as "Sthapathys" (Sanskrit, Tamil = architect/designer) in Tamil Nadu, South India. We wanted to investigate the health of this ancient craft, over 1,000 years old, in the current period of India's rapid economic change and document their lost wax metal casting technology. Was it disappearing? Or, is it thriving?

While travel writers, TV documentarians, art historians, and others have written about the Sthapathys from the village of Swamimalai, ours was the first ethnoarchaeology study. The project surveyed more than 200 casting workshops in the village, created a typology of them, and worked closely with one Sthapathy family workshop. We documented the chain of production, or "chaîne opératoire" from clients ordering sacred bronzes to traditional production methods to the distribution of finished products. The community is more than 1,000 years old and until India's independence in 1947, kept their lost wax casting technology secret.

Crafting wax model of God Garuda for casting

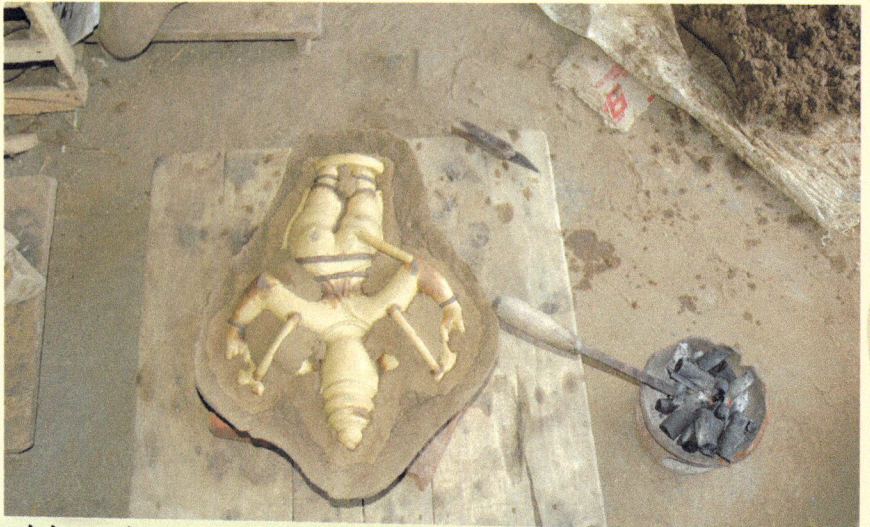

Mold making: Wax icon model with fine clay inner coating and outer of coarse paddy clay

Sthapathys follow sacred Hindu texts (Shilpa Shastras) that explain how religious icons, like the Nataraja or dancing Shiva, should be made. For Sthapathys, these texts were blessed by divinities. Thus, religious icons for temple worship can only be made by members of the Sthapathy community who trace their ancestry back to the Chola Empire (ca. 900–1300 AD). The village of Swamimalai, on the banks of the Kaveri River, has extremely fine clay sediment used in lost-wax bronze production. The wax model (left) of an icon is covered with a layer of this fine clay to retain the details of the wax model. A second layer of coarse clay is then applied to make a mold. When dried and fired, the wax drains out of the mold and is "lost wax." Hot metal is then cast into the mold.

Ethnoarchaeology
The Hereditary Bronze Casters of South India

Casting hot metal into ingot molds scratched into ground

The hot recycled metal is then cast from large 60 kg capacity crucibles into 80 cm long shallow open molds dug into the surface of the backyard of the workshop (left). After 2 weeks of work, the mud cleaner produces 8 ingots or more, each weighing about 10 kg. This recycling process, including the production of ingots, provides important analog models for understanding Iron Age (ca. 1200–500 BCE) metal industries in the Middle East and elsewhere. Our ethnoarchaeology project showed that the traditional metal craft in India is thriving, thanks to the Indian diaspora, who order religious icons for temples around the world. The work also provided new information and models for prehistoric lost-wax metallurgy, recycling, and many other issues.

https://www.academia.edu/10341674/Masters_of_Fire_Hereditary_Bronze_Casters_of_South_India

Ethnoarchaeologists observe things that elude journalists, historians, and others. For example, the importance of metal recycling in traditional metal workshops. In a little-visited part of the Sthapathy workshop, we found a man employed by the Sthapathys to wash sediment from the workshop floor. Each year, the "mud cleaner" spends several weeks extracting metal bits and lumps from the workshop casting floor's 100 m³ of sediment. He also cleans the slag from numerous graphite crucibles left over from a year of work. Once the mud washing and slag cleaning are complete, the sediment and slag are crushed in ground stone mortars and then smelted in furnaces into liquid metal.

Recycling: Mud cleaner extracts metalliferous sediment in washing pool

For archaeologists, the lost-wax method of metal object production has been a puzzle, especially for when metallurgy began. Ethnoarchaeology can provide key analog models to understand how ancient metallurgy worked. The Southern Levant was one of the earliest centers of metal production, in particular, during the Chalcolithic period. At this formative time, open molds were used for chisels and tools, and the lost-wax method for complex objects. Israel's Judean Desert "Cave of the Treasure" had hundreds of complex Chalcolithic metal works, like the twin-ibex mace head on the photocopy in front of Radhakrishna Sthapathy on the left from the original 1960 excavation report. With the Sthapathys, we successfully did experimental archaeology to recreate the lost-wax method probably used during the Chalcolithic period.

Radhakrishna makes Chalcolithic wax model and examines its final casting

THE BOOMER ARCHAEOLOGIST

THOMAS EVAN LEVY

· PHOTO STORY 6 ·

Methoni Bay Marine Archaeology

Cultural Heritage Project, Greece

https://sci-cult.com/digital-underwater-technologies-in-the-methoni-bay-cultural-heritage-project-greece-interdisciplinary-approaches-and-sustainability

THE BOOMER ARCHAEOLOGIST
◦ PHOTO STORY 6 ◦

Research vessel off Greek Peloponnese coast

Our work in Greece, especially the "Methoni Bay Marine Archaeology Cultural Heritage Project," allowed us to establish a 3-tier model for the new Scripps Center for Marine Archaeology at UC San Diego. This includes: shallow marine geophysics, sediment coring for paleoenvironmental reconstructions, and photogrammetry and underwater archaeology excavation to understand how societies responded to climate, environmental, and cultural change. The Methoni Bay, at the tip of Messenia, has cultural heritage sites from prehistory to the present. Especially important is a submerged Middle Bronze Age (2050/2000–1750/1680 BCE) settlement that will provide answers on the rise of Mycenaean civilization, human response to environmental change, and more. Using a cultural heritage asset district model established by the Milken Institute, we created one for Methoni based on maritime culture. I carried out this project with Professors George Papatheodorou and Maria Geraga from the University of Patras, and Elias Spondylis, who first discovered the site.

Shallow marine geophysics (sub-bottom profiler, multi-beam, and side-scan sonar) provided large-scale data concerning the nature of archaeological features on the seafloor and below it. The white track lines in the map to the right show areas intensively surveyed over the submerged Middle Bronze site with marine geophysics spread over ca. 800 m x 400 m. The surface observations show the site to be 1.5 hectares in size; the sub-bottom profile data show it to be more than 14 hectares, perhaps a town.

Track lines over submerged Middle Bronze site

Divers pound core barrel into the sea floor

Tom

Sediment cores provide a wide range of proxy data to reconstruct climate, ecological, and landscape conditions. Sedimentological data such as geochemistry, grain size, and more help reconstruct environmental histories. Biological data such as foraminifera, bivalves, sponges, etc. reveal changes in past ecosystems. Preliminary analyses of cores retrieved underwater at Methoni using the hand coring system shown here inform on the environmental processes that caused the submergence of the site (e.g., tectonics vs. sea-level rise), the geomorphological setting of the site when it was occupied some 3,500 years ago and more.

Methoni Bay Marine Archaeology
Cultural Heritage Project, Greece

Diver swims over stone foundation of Bronze Age circular feature

The architectural remains of the Middle Bronze Age settlement spread over the seafloor are easily visible to divers and even from boats, as the site is 4 to 6 m below the surface of crystal-clear water. Here, I scuba dive over a large, approx. 6 m diameter, stone circle at Methoni. This may be the foundation of a granary, tomb, or other structure. The challenge is how to accurately map a huge site with intricate architectural features.

Underwater photogrammetry, the extraction of 3D information from georeferenced photographs, provides a quick and accurate method for mapping and recording underwater archaeology sites. To map the massive submerged settlement at Methoni, we developed a motorized camera rig powered by an electric scuba scooter that housed 3 high-definition DSLR cameras that fired automatically with a modular intervalometer unit. A 25 x 25 m grid was established over the site, and a diver would swim transects collecting image data. The diver operated the system over submerged archaeological remains and reference scale bar.

Photogrammetry with underwater scuba scooter

Map made of Bronze Age circular structures on Methoni sea floor

The Methoni project demonstrated the utility of combining marine geophysics, sediment coring, and photogrammetry for understanding the complexity of the submerged Middle Bronze settlement. Maps of the site (left) aid in the documentation of this unique cultural heritage site and its integration into related regional efforts in this part of Greece.

https://sci-cult.com/digital-underwater-technologies-in-the-methoni-bay-cultural-heritage-project-greece-interdisciplinary-approaches-and-sustainability

THE BOOMER ARCHAEOLOGIST

THOMAS EVAN LEVY

• PHOTO STORY 7 •

Deep-Time Holocene Coastal Adaptation

Israel and the Earliest Tsunami

https://www.youtube.com/watch?v=z6DssjtQJaE&t=18s
https://journals.plos.org/plosone/article?id=10.1371/journal.pone.0243619

THE BOOMER ARCHAEOLOGIST
· PHOTO STORY 7 ·

Drone paths over Dor

The University of Haifa-UC San Diego "Deep-time study of Holocene Coastal Adaptation Israel" project combines marine geophysics, sediment coring, underwater excavation, and photogrammetry to answer human-paleoenvironmental questions. Since 2017, we have produced many studies and publications. Of great public interest is the identification of the earliest documented Holocene tsunami event, between 7910–7290 BC, from the Eastern Mediterranean at Dor, Israel.

3D View Dor

The small "pocket bay" to the south of Tel Dor (figure B) provides a unique setting for capturing the recent geological history of Israel's coast. How did human societies respond to the catastrophic tsunami event?

Diver at Dor excavates with hydraulic dredge

To understand relative sea-level change and reconstruct coastal adjustments, submerged archaeological sites provide key data points for measuring these changes. Underwater survey and excavation provide the context of nearshore human adaptations. The Carmel Coast contains evidence of submerged sites from the Pre-Pottery Neolithic (ca. 6960 BCE) to the recent past. For the tsunami study, new Neolithic sites were discovered and sampled with excavation.

Deep-time Holocene Coastal Adaptation
Israel and the Earliest Tsunami

Geoprobe drill operates in Dor South Bay

Extracting undisturbed sediment cores with clear layering is key to making accurate paleoenvironmental interpretations. High-quality continuous samples require high-quality sediment sampling tools. One of the best is the "Geoprobe" direct push subsurface sampling technology that pushes a metal and plastic sampling tube into the ground without disturbing the subsurface layers, easily reaching depths of over 15 m — perfect for investigating Holocene deposits. For the nearshore and coastal plain research along the Carmel coast, our team made 4 coring expeditions, collecting hundreds of meters of ancient sediments using the Geoprobe shown here.

The geomorphological investigations of the Carmel coast cores were spearheaded by Gilad Shtienberg, my postdoc from 2018–2023. Using the "Big Wall" at UC San Diego's Qualcomm Institute, a tiled display environment with 4 rows of 8 displays for a total of 32 narrow-bezel LCD displays with a 55" screen diagonal (and up to 66 million pixels on the wall) — researchers share data in real time. Here, the F3 unit anomaly is shown that clearly indicates the tsunami intrusion on the paleo-beach at Dor, between 7910–7290 BC.

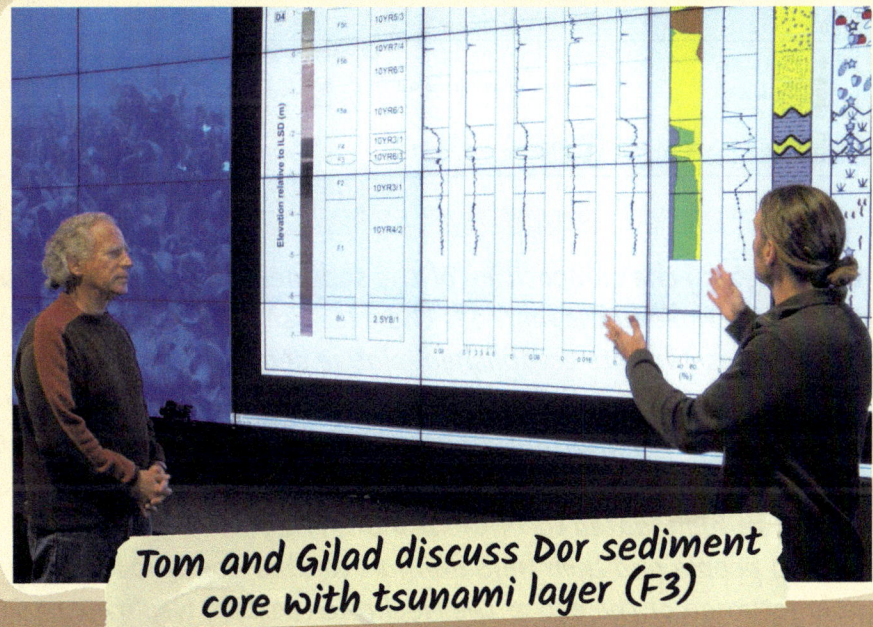

Tom and Gilad discuss Dor sediment core with tsunami layer (F3)

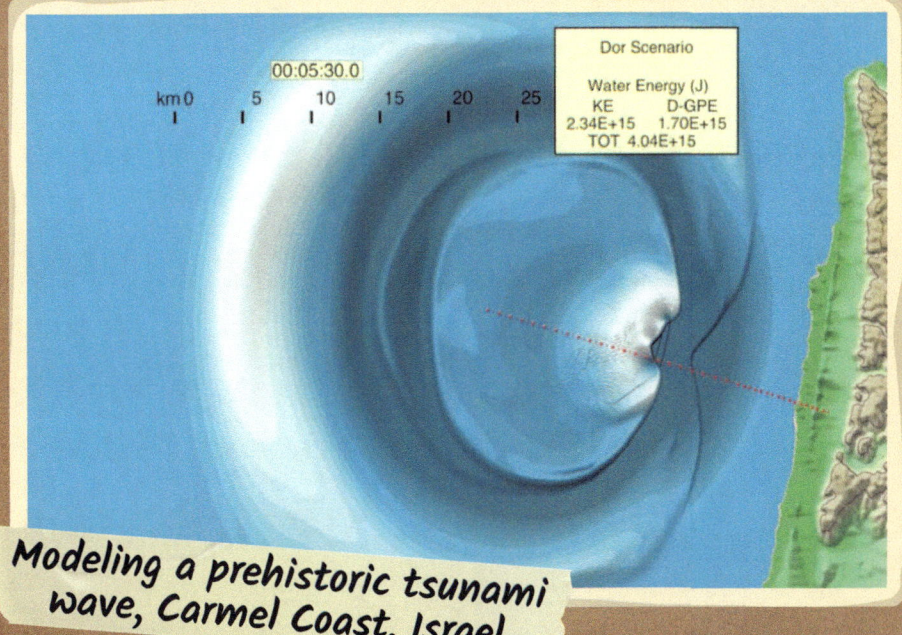

Modeling a prehistoric tsunami wave, Carmel Coast, Israel

Working with geophysicist Steven Ward, our team made an animated model of the early Neolithic tsunami off Israel's Carmel coast. The seismically-generated tsunami scenario was created by pairing an earthquake with wave simulations. The earthquake trigger for the early Neolithic tsunami may have been a major earthquake in the Jordan Valley that activated a marine landslide off the Carmel coast that caused the huge wave.

THE BOOMER ARCHAEOLOGIST
• PHOTO STORY 7 •

Dor Holocene sediment characteristics and sea levels

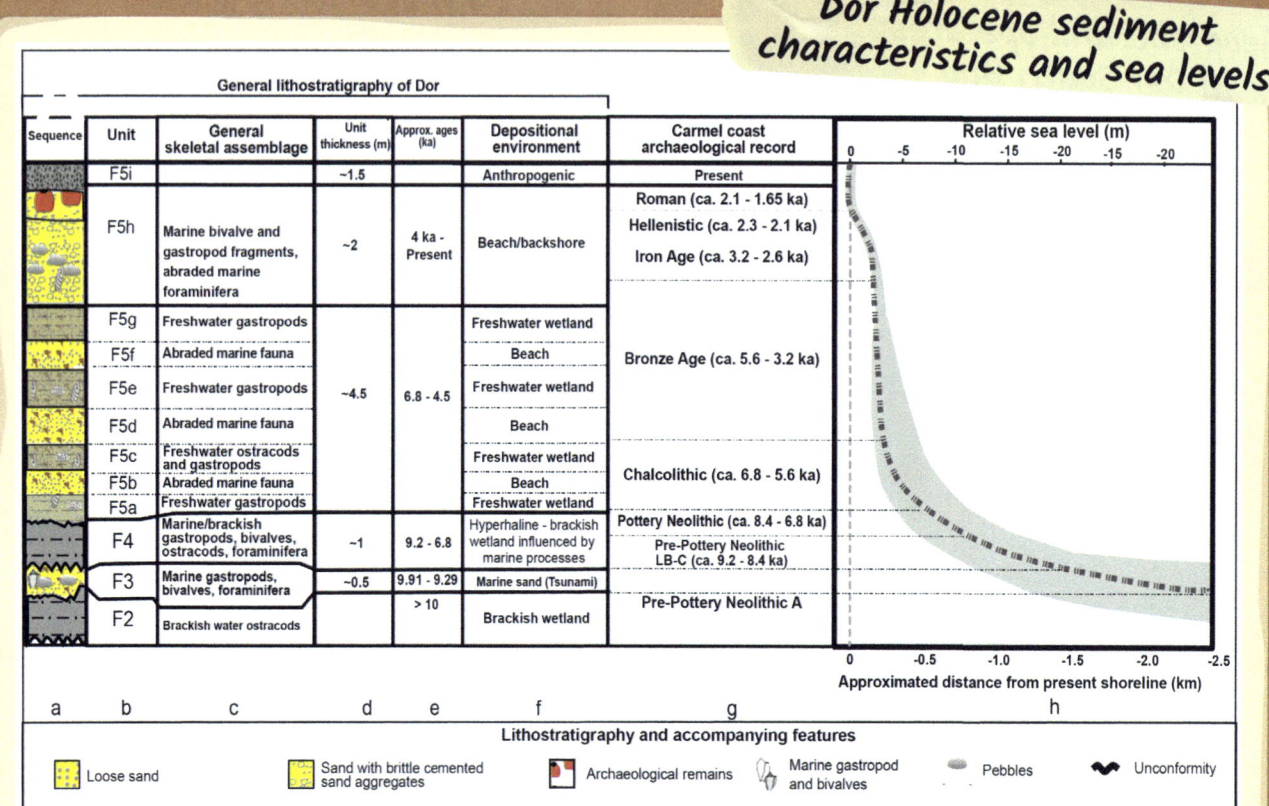

By analyzing the composition of the sediment layer's cores around Dor's South Bay, dating them with radiometric methods (here we use OSL — Optical Stimulated Luminescence), and linking these data to established relative sea-level curves, it is possible to define changing environments. During the Pre-Pottery Neolithic A period, the silty, brackish wetland environment was interrupted with the tsunami event (Unit F3) that left marine shells and other non-wetland material, brought from a minimum distance of 1.5 km and a wave over 16 m high, dated to 7910–7290 BC. The tsunami destroyed the nearshore ecosystem, forcing people and their herd animals to abandon this formerly rich environment. Settlers only returned at the end of the Neolithic (Pottery Neolithic period), some 1,500 years later.

THOMAS EVAN LEVY

Lily and Uncle Tom on Phone Call

LONDON, UK, SEPTEMBER 2, 2024

HI UNCLE TOM, IT'S BEEN A WHILE SINCE WE SPOKE. YOU MENTIONED IN A WHATAPP MESSAGE THAT YOU WANTED TO ADD ANOTHER CHAPTER TO THE MEMOIR. WHY NOW?

SAN DIEGO, CALIFORNIA

HI LILY, GREAT TO HEAR YOU. AFTER OCTOBER 7 LAST YEAR AND THE HAMAS TERRORISTS' INVASION OF SOUTHERN ISRAEL, EVERYTHING CHANGED FOR THE JEWISH COMMUNITY; NOT ONLY IN ISRAEL, BUT AROUND THE WORLD. WITH ALL THE UNEASINESS, I COULDN'T END MY MEMOIR WITH THE NOTION OF GRATITUDE; IT IS IMPORTANT TO REFLECT ON WHERE WE ARE AT NOW. HERE WE GO...

THE BOOMER ARCHAEOLOGIST

THOMAS EVAN LEVY

• POSTSCRIPT •

October 7, 2023

THE BOOMER ARCHAEOLOGIST
◦ POSTSCRIPT ◦

In July 2023, I completed my graphic memoir and was finalizing its production with my graphic designer, BhaveshKumar Suru, in India. Having recently retired, I completed the memoir with the notion of gratitude. Retirement meant no more teaching, no more crazy faculty meetings. The opportunity to enjoy the fruits of a wonderful career topped off new research in underwater archaeology, coupled with more time with Alina.

Post-retirement research was looking great. By October 2023, the last year of our +$1 million UCSD-University of Haifa Koret Foundation grant would be topped off with an underwater excavation off the Carmel coast.

October 7, 2023

On October 6, Alina dropped me off at the San Diego Intl. Airport; we hugged, and she wished me luck for a great expedition.

My connecting flight to Israel was at the JFK Intl. Airport. Settling into my Delta Comfort seat, I introduced myself to my neighbor — Nir, a young man on leave from the IDF. By takeoff time at 11:45 p.m., Nir was ashen-faced and frantically texting with his brother, who worked in the Israeli embassy in Washington DC.

In real time, the texts said that Israel was being invaded by a Hamas terrorist army of thousands, and hundreds of Israelis were dead. It was the worst mass killing of Jews since the Holocaust during WWII. It was 7:45 a.m. on October 7 in Israel as we took off, and the Hamas onslaught was only a few hours old.

As we flew into Ben Gurion Airport, Nir and I debated whether this October 7 surprise attack was worse than the one on Yom Kippur — almost 50 years to the day earlier. It was only after landing and learning of the magnitude of the Hamas invasion inside southern Israel, in towns and kibbutzim, and the atrocities they carried out against innocent women, men, children, and grandparents that this October 7 was beginning to seem worse than the Yom Kippur War of 1973.

I picked up my rental car around 6:30 p.m., and began to drive north through Tel Aviv on the Ayalon Highway toward Nahsholim, our project headquarters on the Carmel Coast.

THE BOOMER ARCHAEOLOGIST
- POSTSCRIPT -

OCTOBER 7 EVENING WHILE DRIVING THROUGH TEL AVIV

October 7, 2023

Suddenly there was a giant traffic jam. Then I saw hundreds of people jumping out of their cars, running for cover, and throwing themselves on the ground with their hands over their necks. We were under a rocket attack, and the Iron Dome was shooting the incoming projectiles out of the sky. After 10 minutes, everyone piled back into their cars, and we resumed driving north.

WELL-ARMED HAMAS TERRORIST INSIDE ISRAEL ON OCTOBER 7

OCTOBER 7: YOUNG PEOPLE FLEEING HAMAS TERRORISTS WHO SLAUGHTERED 364, RAPED MANY OF THE WOMEN, AND CAPTURED HOSTAGES AT THE SUPERNOVA SUKKOT MUSIC FESTIVAL NEAR KIBBUTZ REIM, 5 KM EAST OF GAZA.

In the morning of October 8, I walked to the beach at Dor to meet my research partner, Assaf Yasur-Landau; diving officer, Amir Yurman; and the University of Haifa team.

Everyone was reeling from the chaos of the past 24 hours, trying to understand what was happening. Terrorists were still inside Israel, and the army and security services, after totally dropping the ball that allowed some 6,000 armed terrorists and Gazan citizens to burst through the Gaza

THE BOOMER ARCHAEOLOGIST
∘ POSTSCRIPT ∘

border to wreak havoc in the south, were finally eliminating most of the infiltrators.

But the army was inexplicably late. People were slaughtered in their homes. And why didn't those Israelis living along the Gaza border have weapons in their homes? Even in America, my dad, who had helped liberate Dachau, advocated that Jews must be armed.

Prior to October 7, Israel was getting close to establishing ties with Saudi Arabia, the Arab world's most important country. Commentators on the news suggested Hamas, a proxy for the Islamic Republic of Iran, attacked Israel to destroy these peace overtures.

Using what I have called "archaeo-diplomacy," my approach to having worked in the Arab world for decades, we were close to making a major Moroccan-Israel-USA project. Unfortunately, the chaos and uncertainty of the past 24 hours led Assaf and me to contact 2 distinguished Moroccan archaeologists who were about to fly to Israel to work with us. We told them to cancel their flights. They wrote us remarkably touching, sympathetic emails in support of Israel. As of this writing, our collaboration is on hold until the dust settles.

How was it possible that Israel's esteemed army, its security services, and the government were caught by surprise? These are some of Israel's most important institutions that

October 7, 2023

broke the unwritten social contract with the people of Israel and their country.

My dear friend, the noted Czech Egyptologist, Mirek Barta, studied the rise and fall of civilizations. Mirek has shown, among other things, that failure of the social contract can lead to civilizational collapse. Could this be happening in Israel? After the war, Israel will initiate a commission of inquiry to understand the security failures leading to October 7.

Prior to October 7, Israeli society was in turmoil over the issue of judicial reform for almost a year. Tens of thousands would protest every Saturday evening after Shabbat, both

ROEY'S IDF RECONNAISSANCE UNIT SOMEWHERE IN THE GAZA STRIP, OCTOBER 2023–FEBRUARY 2024

for and against the issue. Was Israel tearing itself apart? Some thought this was a moment of internal weakness and that it encouraged Hamas to attack Israel.

Amazingly, overnight, on October 8, all the Israeli protest groups disbanded and morphed into many well-organized volunteer organizations to help in the war effort against Hamas. During the chaos of those first days of the war, I could feel the unity of the country as we tried to carry out our expedition.

One of Assaf's talented Israeli graduate students, Roey Nickelsberg, had recently moved to the USA with his American wife. As part of his PhD, we worked closely with Roey on the Habonim underwater Neolithic site that we published in the prestigious British journal ANTIQUITY.

After October 7, like so many young Israelis, Roey rushed to make his way back to Israel. This was some days before Israel invaded Gaza. Roey then served in the Gaza Strip for 3 ½ months with his reconnaissance unit, a part of an armored division.

Late at night on October 7, I checked into the Nahsholim Seaside Resort, my residence in Israel when working with Assaf and the University of Haifa team. By breakfast time on October 8, the hotel dining room was filled up with over 150 refugees from Kibbutz Karmiya from the Gaza region.

October 7, 2023

OCTOBER 7: AN ISRAELI RESIDENT IN THE NORTHERN NEGEV TOWN OF OFAKIM RUNS IN FRONT OF BURNING CARS DURING THE BATTLE WITH HAMAS TERRORISTS WHO KILLED 53 INNOCENT PEOPLE IN OFAKIM. MY CHALCOLITHIC TEMPLE EXCAVATIONS AT GILAT, CARRIED OUT IN THE EARLY '90s, ARE NEXT TO OFAKIM.

That morning, I walked down the beach to our base camp at Moshav Dor and found Assaf, science diving officer Amir Yurman, and our Haifa team loading the pump boat with excavation equipment.

I had recruited 2 awesome American divers as volunteers — John Schedel and Duke Pigott. I knew Duke as a fellow member of The Explorers Club and found them in the water, helping our team.

After work, I started to call many of my friends throughout Israel. Since Alina and I left Israel in 1992, I have visited the country every year, either for work or to spend time with friends. The chaos in the country led all my friends to say that, unfortunately, this was not a good time to meet up.

THE BOOMER ARCHAEOLOGIST
◦ POSTSCRIPT ◦

Concerned about the hundreds of rockets being launched into Israel from Gaza, the continued presence of terrorists inside southern Israel, and increasing attacks by Hezbollah from Lebanon, Israelis wanted to simply go to work and return home. Many of their spouses and children were being called up for the army. Amir's 20-year-old son had just been rescued from the development town of Ofakim, under savage Hamas attack; and his 23-year-old daughter was called up for IDF reserve duty on the Lebanon border.

OCTOBER 10, 2023: PACKING UP OUR MARINE ARCHAEOLOGY EQUIPMENT ON THE BEACH AT DOR AND POSTPONING THE PROJECT DUE TO THE POST-OCTOBER 7 CHAOS.

October 7, 2023

Beginning October 7, Israel was besieged and in chaos. International flights in and out of Israel were cancelled. More refugees from the Kibbutzim near Gaza were pouring into Israel's hotels, including mine.

My friend, Yitzhak Marmelstein, an expert in drones, evacuated his family from Ashkelon to the north and called me to say that I should leave Israel.

On the third day of the war, I walked down the beach to meet Assaf, Amir, and the team. We all spoke at the same time, saying that we had to postpone the project until more quiet times.

The magnitude of Hamas' crimes, including at the Nova Music Festival where over 300 young people were slaughtered and many young women were raped, was not yet broadcast on the Israeli news.

With no project and no family in Israel, my hotel filling up with evacuees from the Hamas invasion, and all my dear friends consumed with the survival of their own families, I felt that I had nothing to do in Israel at the time. My family and home were in California.

50 years ago, I was determined to come to Israel from Greece during the Yom Kippur War to volunteer (milking cows). In the late '70s until the early '90s, Alina and I were totally part of the Israel project. Now, at 70 years old, I

THE BOOMER ARCHAEOLOGIST
· POSTSCRIPT ·

was anxious to leave Israel before the doors shut. I wasn't happy with my decision.

After work, I invited Duke and John to my Nahsholim hotel room so we could try to book flights. With Ben Gurion Airport basically closed, the only way out was overland through Jordan. Assaf treated us to a taxi from Haifa to the Beth Shean border crossing. I hadn't been back to Jordan since 2014. We were picked up on the Jordanian side by Sultan,

TOM AND MIREK BÁRTA OUTSIDE THE GIZA PYRAMID FIELDS, CAIRO, OCTOBER 2023, AT THE RESEARCH CENTER OF ESTEEMED AMERICAN EGYPTOLOGIST, MARK LEHNER.

October 7, 2023

a friend of Duke's from the Tell el-Hammam excavation where he had worked for years.

It felt good and bizarre to be in "peaceful" Jordan, and Sultan treated us to an amazing lunch near Jerash on the road to Amman. It dawned on me that since arriving in Israel on October 7, I hadn't eaten well, so having the typical Jordanian Mansaf meal with numerous salads was very special.

We drove to the American Center of Research (ACOR), located in the Tla'Ali area of Amman, where I paid for our accommodation. As Delta Air Lines has their major Middle East hub in Cairo, Duke and I decided to fly to Egypt the next day. That evening, I met my old friend and colleague Mohammad Najjar for dinner. We tried to understand where things were headed.

While in Israel, I had been in touch with my friend Mirek, who invited us to visit his excavations at Abusir, near the Great Pyramids. When I told Alina about our travel plans, she said that I was out of my mind.

I had never been to Egypt. As Mirek promised to pick us up at the Cairo Intl. Airport and look after us, I felt good about the stopover. We stayed at the amazing Meena Hotel near the Pyramids. The next day, Friday, Hamas called for a day of rage throughout the Arab world. Little did I know that when I returned to the USA, my own college campus would turn out to be an ongoing center of pro-Hamas rage.

THE BOOMER ARCHAEOLOGIST
POSTSCRIPT

Lily and Uncle Tom on Phone Call

LONDON, SEPTEMBER 11, 2024

"HI UNCLE TOM — HAPPY BIRTHDAY! WOW! IT'S REMARKABLE HOW YOU WERE IN ISRAEL THE DAY THE HAMAS TERRORISTS INVADED ISRAEL. WHAT A CRAZY STORY. ARE WE DONE NOW?"

SAN DIEGO, CALIFORNIA

"HI LILY, THANKS! NOT QUITE. I MUST EXPLAIN A LITTLE BIT ABOUT THE UNFORTUNATE ANTISEMITIC TURN OF EVENTS AT MY HOME UNIVERSITY AND OTHER DEVELOPMENTS. IT'S AN EXAMPLE OF WHAT HAS HAPPENED ACROSS THE USA AND IN DIFFERENT ELITE INSTITUTIONS THROUGHOUT THE WESTERN WORLD; THEN WE ARE DONE."

October 7, 2023

Globalizing the Intifada — UCSD

MAY 1, 2024: PRO-HAMAS MASKED STUDENTS AND THEIR SUPPORTERS ESTABLISHED AN "ENCAMPMENT" AT MY HOME UC SAN DIEGO CAMPUS.

While I was in Israel, the strangest thing happened at UC San Diego and campuses across the USA on October 8, just hours after the Hamas invasion and atrocities. Israel had not yet started their full-scale military assault on Gaza. Pro-Hamas demonstrations erupted on our campus and at 140 elite US university campuses in 45 states. Alina went to UCSD for the first pro-Israel demo to show support for our beleaguered Jewish students.

THE BOOMER ARCHAEOLOGIST
• POSTSCRIPT •

How could American students show support for Hamas, a US State Department-designated terrorist organization, which had just invaded Israel — devastating towns and villages, murdering some 1200 Israeli and other nationals, raping, decapitating, taking away 250 adults, children, and babies for hostages? Who recorded their actions with GoPro cameras and celebrated their terrorism on social media with their friends and family in Gaza? How did we get here?

On returning home, I had that same awful feeling as in 1972, when my college friends celebrated the killing of Israeli athletes at the Munich Olympics. Only now, the scale of the atrocities and the hatred against Jews and Israel was well-organized — supported by thousands of students, outside agitators, and many faculty members across the USA, including on my own campus.

Protests went on for months and continue as of this writing. In early May 2024, a pro-Hamas, anti-Israel encampment was established near the UCSD Geisel Library, where masked students and outside agitators carried out daily Islamic prayers, had weapons, disrupted free movement on campus, and intimidated Jewish students and faculty. After 5 days of administration interactions with the mob, UC San Diego Chancellor Pradeep Khosla courageously called the police, who removed the illegal encampment. While this sparked members of the faculty senate to call for his censure and removal from office, a faculty vote supported the chancellor. I actively supported Khosla.

October 7, 2023

UCSD Levantine Archaeology Laboratory

Professor Thomas E. Levy

Norma Kershaw Chair
in the
Archaeology of Ancient Israel and Neighboring Lands

Israel admits to organ thefts

FEBRUARY 28, 2024: MY LAB AT UCSD

From 2021–2024, the Koret Foundation funded a UCSD–University of Haifa project, which was annually targeted by the UCSD Graduate and Professional Student Association for the BDS movement (Boycott, Divestment, Sanctions). Things got worse after October 7, when my lab was targeted and plastered with inflammatory blood libel pages with the aim of intimidating me and my students.

THE BOOMER ARCHAEOLOGIST
• POSTSCRIPT •

The reasons for student rage on US campuses are many; here are a few:

Students were locked up for several years during the COVID-19 pandemic and primed to explode when offered an ideology of revolutionary freedom. A university culture evolved based on identity politics where Diversity, Equity, and Inclusion (DEI) policy has been baked into university administration, fostering racial tension and contributing to antisemitism on college campuses. The result is an abandonment of strengthening American group identity and the pitting of perceived BIPOC (Black, Indigenous, and people of color) against perceived white people.

Underlying DEI is Critical Race Theory (CRT), based on the assumption that systemic racism is central to America. For CRT, Jews are classified as white, resulting in erasing the notion of Jews as an oppressed minority (a fact since the Exodus over 3,000 years ago!) to an archetypal white oppressor group.

Then there are the Marxist theories taught to the students in the arts, humanities, and social sciences, based on the concept of oppressor-oppressed. The college classes always have a lecture or more castigating Israel and Zionism as typical of post-colonial theory, where democratic Israel is

October 7, 2023

the oppressor, and Palestinians, including terrorists, are the oppressed.

By suppressing alternative views on campuses, most students at elite research universities are uniformed. As many non-mainstream journalists have reported, when students shout, "From the river to the sea, Palestine will be free," many have no idea what river (Jordan) or sea (Mediterranean) they are shouting for. They have no understanding that Zionism is the liberation movement of the Jewish people; that, along with India, Israel is the most successful post-colonial state established after WWII; that Israel is the size of New Jersey, ethnically diverse with a "brown" majority; that Jews as a people are not "white" (see my teen-penned poem earlier, on page 59); that there is only one Jewish state and 23 Islamic states, and 49 countries where Muslims represent more than half the population, and more.

My memoir traces how these troubling social trends developed on one elite university campus — mine. ✡

THE BOOMER ARCHAEOLOGIST
· POSTSCRIPT ·

"Dream Palace of the Arabs" — Gaza 2024

"Dream Palace of the Arabs" is a book by the brilliant Near Eastern Studies professor, Fouad Ajami, the late American of Lebanese Shiite background who had an insider understanding of the Middle East. In his book, Ajami showed how over the past 100 years, Arab intellectuals and leaders became dazzled by evolving ideologies such as Nasser's pan-Arabism and Islamic fundamentalism. The goal was always to resurrect the great periods of Arab history, and it always ended with tragedy for the Arab masses.

Hamas (Islamic Resistance Movement), a Sunni Arab group, and Hezbollah (Party of God), a Shiite Arab group, have embraced the leadership of the Shiite non-Arab Islamic Republic of Iran, with ultimate authority vested in a supreme leader so that a new caliphate can be created.

October 7, 2023

They serve as Iran's proxies aimed at destroying Israel. By hiding behind Gaza's civilians, Hamas has got thousands of Palestinian civilians killed; with a new "Dream Palace" smoldering on the ruins of Gaza in the hope of building the caliphate. ✡

THE BOOMER ARCHAEOLOGIST
· POSTSCRIPT ·

Back to Israel: May 2024

Day 237 of the Gaza War: Assaf and I decided that 7 months into the war, the situation along the Lebanon border and in Gaza was quiet enough to try to resume our underwater excavation — exactly where we left off after October 7.

The goal was to return to the Dor/Tantura lagoon, where we identified 3 Iron Age cargos, spanning the 11th to 7th centuries BCE. I contacted Duke Pigott to see if he wanted to return to Israel, despite the current war. Duke jumped at the idea and arrived in Israel a week after me. When I arrived at the Nahsholim hotel, the refugees from Kibbutz Karmia were still there.

October 7, 2023

As a fellow of The Explorers Club (TEC), I thought it would be important to apply for a TEC expedition flag. Carrying a flag reflects an impressive history of courage and accomplishment; hundreds of expeditions led by club members have carried the flag since 1918, including the Apollo 11 moon landing in July 1969.

Our Flag (#151) expedition had awesome results. We excavated the 7th century BCE Phoenician cargo with anchors, amphorae, iron ingots/blooms, and more! This is a key data point to understand Phoenician connectivity in the Mediterranean post-Bronze Age world.

THE BOOMER ARCHAEOLOGIST
◦ POSTSCRIPT ◦

When do I end this memoir?

Day 331 of Gaza War, September 1, 2024: I'm ending my memoir today. We learned that 6 Israeli hostages — after being held in Hamas captivity for over 10 months — were starved, kept in suffocating unlit Gaza tunnels, and brutally executed by the Hamas terrorists with multiple bullet wounds. They were found in a tunnel under Rafah, in the southern Gaza Strip. They include Hersh Goldberg-Polin, a 23-year-old Israeli-American; a beautiful 24-year-old pilates teacher named Eden Yerushalmi, starved to 79 pounds; 40-year-old Carmel Gat; Almog Sarusi; 32-year-old Russian-Israeli Alexander Lobanov; and 25-year-old Ori Danino. All were abducted from the Nova Music festival, except for Carmel, who was taken from Kibbutz Be'eri. There are still more than 60 living hostages and 35 corpses thought to be in Gaza as of this writing.

The tragic deaths of these young captives have torn Israeli society into 2 — the second time since October 7. The cohesion of Jewish and Israeli society rests on the notion that כל המציל נפש אחת כאילו הציל עולם ומלואו —

"Whoever saves one soul is as if he saved the whole world" (Mishna, Sanhedrin 4:5). Probably half of the Israeli public now argues for a deal with the terrorists, at any cost, to safely bring the hostages home. The other half argues that to give in to terror now will mean losing the war,

October 7, 2023

sacrificing the more than 2,000 Israelis dead from this war for nothing, and that the terrorists will be emboldened by perceived Israeli weakness to carry out future attacks. After almost a year, the war continues and will probably intensify soon with Iran's better-armed proxy, Hezbollah, which has displaced more than 70,000 Israelis from their homes in northern Israel.

ALINA AT PRO-ISRAEL DEMO AT UCSD, END OF 2024 ACADEMIC YEAR.

THE BOOMER ARCHAEOLOGIST
◦ POSTSCRIPT ◦

No one knows how this will end. However, one thing is clear: when the war ends, the Israelis and Palestinians will still be there. Will the Palestinians say this war, which Hamas started, was worth it? As my dear friend Yossi Klein Halevi writes to his Palestinian neighbors, the 2 sides must accept the premise "that 2 indigenous peoples share this land and the right to self-determination."

"Jewish history and world history grind me between them like two grindstones, sometimes to a powder." This is part of a poem* by the Israeli poet, Yehuda Amichai, that beautifully captures the essence of the Jewish experience.

Like all proud Jews, I have been fortunate to be a part of that history — one that has both universalistic and particularistic dimensions. We have been debating these since Talmudic times.

I Wasn't One of the Six Million: And What Is My Life Span? Open Closed Open by Yehuda Amichai, 2000.

As the story presented here shows, I have been blessed to have been born in a post-WWII America full of opportunities, one that has mostly celebrated its Jewish citizens.

At the same time, I have been lucky to have experienced being part of Israel, with all its joys and complexities. What Yossi** describes as "being part of an indigenous people that is being repatriated." This is my story. For

October 7, 2023

Palestinians, Yossi explains, "I'm part of a colonialist wave that's threatening their sense of home." I continue to believe we have to work to reconcile these realities.

    **Interview May 12, 2011
    On Being with Krista Tippett
    Yossi Klein Halevi
    Thin Places, Thick Realities

Having excavated grinding stones and other artifacts in the deserts of the American Southwest and in the Holy Land my entire adult life, I continue to experience the universalistic and particularistic aspects of my identity with pride and tension. It never ends. ✡

THE BOOMER ARCHAEOLOGIST

NOVEMBER 2023: MY MOM AND I CELEBRATE THE PUBLICATION OF MY FESTSCHRIFT AT HER ASSISTED LIVING FACILITY IN OUR SAN DIEGO NEIGHBORHOOD. MOM PASSED AWAY TWO MONTHS LATER AT THE AGE OF 97 AND A HALF. A LIFE WELL-LIVED.